First published 2021

(c) 2021 Dominic Salles

CW00447912

Dominic Salles still lives in Swindon, with his workaholic wife Deirdre. His jiu-jitsu-loving ex-engineer son, Harry, has moved to Shoreditch and lives on the site of Shakespeare's first theatre. Destiny. Bob, the 16.5-year-old rescue dog still refuses to die.

His daughter Jess is educating students in Wales because, now Brexit is done, Brussels isn't stepping in to help the Welsh any more. She is learning to surf. Destiny rides again – I am going snowboarding for three months in January 2022, surfing the snow. I have paid!

His sister Jacey is famous for her Spanish accent, on your TV screens, and is also filming in Wales. She would be hilarious in her own YouTube channel. His 2006 Prius has just died and been rein*car*nated (who writes these puns?) as a 2019 Prius.

His YouTube channel, Mr Salles Teaches English, will one day earn him a living – perhaps when exams return. Your cloud is my silver lining.

Other Grade 9 Guides by Mr Salles

Language

The Mr Salles Guide to **100% at AQA GCSE English Language**
The Mr Salles Guide to **Awesome Story Writing**
The Mr Salles Quick Guide to **Awesome Description**
The Mr Salles Quick Guide to **Grammar, Punctuation and Spelling**
The Mr Salles Ultimate Guide to **Persuasive Writing**

Literature

The Mr Salles Guide to **GCSE English Literature**
Study Guide Mr Salles Analyses **Jekyll and Hyde**
The Mr Salles Ultimate Guide to **Macbeth**
The Mr Salles Guide to **An Inspector Calls**
The Mr Salles Ultimate Guide to **A Christmas Carol**

All are available on Amazon

Contents Page

How to Use This Guide   **Page 3**
Part 1 – The Quick Guide   **Page 4**
Summary of the Play   **Page 5**
    The Prologue   **Page 10**
    Act 1 Scene 1   **Page 10**
    Act 1 Scene 2   **Page 12**
    Act 1 Scene 3   **Page 13**
    Act 1 Scene 4   **Page 14**
    Act 1 Scene 5   **Page 15**
    Act 2 Scene 1 and Prologue   **Page 18**
    Act 2 Scene 2   **Page 20**
    Act 2 Scene 3   **Page 23**
    Act 2 Scene 4   **Page 25**
    Act 2 Scene 5   **Page 26**
    Act 2 Scene 6   **Page 27**
    Act 3 Scene 1   **Page 27**
    Act 3 Scene 2   **Page 30**
    Act 3 Scene 3   **Page 32**
    Act 3 Scene 4   **Page 34**
    Act 3 Scene 5   **Page 35**
    Act 4 Scene 1   **Page 37**
    Act 4 Scene 2   **Page 39**
    Act 4 Scene 3   **Page 40**
    Act 4 Scene 4   **Page 40**
    Act 4 Scene 5   **Page 40**
    Act 5 Scene 1   **Page 42**
    Act 5 Scene 2   **Page 43**
    Act 5 Scene 3   **Page 44**

Part 2 – Context   **Page 48**
Top Ten Context of 1597   **Page 48**
Top Ten Changes to Brooke's Poem   **Page 54**
Top Ten Context of Shakespeare's Life   **Page 56**
Top Ten Facts About Verona   **Page 58**

Part 3 – Themes   **Page 59**
Top Ten Themes   **Page 59**
Top Ten Love Quotes   **Page 62**
Top Ten Fate Quotes   **Page 64**
Top Ten Sex Quotes   **Page 67**
Top Ten Death Quotes   **Page 70**
Top Ten Symbols   **Page 73**

20/02

Part 4 – Form and Structure   **Page 82**
Top Ten Examples of Impulsiveness and Hubris   **Page 82**
Top Ten Structural Questions   **Page 84**
Top Ten Facts About Iambic Pentameter and Free Verse   **Page 85**
Top Ten Features of Greek Tragedy   **Page 88**
Top Twenty Reversals of Fortune – Peripeteias   **Page 92**
Top Ten Facts About Sonnets   **Page 93**
Top Ten Interesting Questions Asked on Google   **Page 94**

Part 5 – How to Write an Essay   **Page 97**
Top Ten Exam Questions   **Page 97**
Top Ten Implications for Your Revision   **Page 100**
Top Ten Thesis Statements   **Page 101**
Top Ten Romeo Quotes   **Page 102**
Top Ten Juliet Quotes   **Page 105**
Top Ten Nurse Quotes   **Page 110**
Top Ten Mercutio Quotes   **Page 115**
Top Ten Tybalt Quotes   **Page 118**
Top Ten Friar Quotes   **Page 122**
Top Ten Benvolio Quotes   **Page 126**
Top Ten Capulet Quotes   **Page 129**
Top Ten Lady Capulet Quotes   **Page 134**
Top Ten Lord and Lady Montague Quotes   **Page 138**
Top Ten Prince Quotes   **Page 140**
Top Ten Minor Character Quotes   **Page 142**

How to Use This Guide

This is my first guide written for all students, even if you are currently getting really low grades. It will deliver top grades!

My next-door neighbour took his GCSEs in 2021, the year of home learning and Covid school closures, and students returning to schools to sit loads of assessments instead of formal exams. He had no interest in English and was expected to get a grade 4. His grandmother decided to teach him English and was surprised to find I write revision guides. I told her that every student can do brilliantly at literature, because it is just knowing stuff. My guides would do the trick, I promised, because they had much more interesting stuff in them than the bitesize guides published elsewhere.

So he achieved a grade 7 in literature and this was his highest grade.

But here's the problem. He didn't read a single guide. Not one. His grandparents did. And then they taught him what was in them. They told me they loved the guides. But still, I felt terrible about this.

He hated reading, and wasn't too happy about studying hard. And that's the problem I've tried to address with this guide. If you love Literature, you will get a top grade by reading the guide. If you hate English, just read **The Quick Guide** at the start, in **Part 1**, or just revise the main characters in **Part 5.**

Part 1 – The Quick Guide

You'll find Part 1 is short. 45 pages. Yet it contains **10 grade 7-9 ideas** for *each* scene. So, no matter what the extract is in your question, you can get a top grade. If you *only* read this part, you will be able to get at least a grade 7.

Part 2 – Context

All top grades depend on you understanding Shakespeare's purpose. If you'd like grades 8 and 9, here's all the context about Shakespeare and his time which will help you smash those grades.

Part 3 – Themes

This is also where you will find the **10 themes** of the play explained.

Part 4 – Form and Structure

All exam boards want you to write about **"form and structure"** for grades 8 and 9. Find out what you need to know.

Part 5 – How to Write an Essay

Here you will find each character analysed with **10 quotations each**. Each section works as a Grade 9 essay on each character.

You'll also find **10 thesis statements**, one for every exam question.

And **10 words to use in every essay**, which will guarantee you top grades.

Part 1: The Quick Guide

Summary of the Play

Act 1 Scene 1

Sunday morning. A third brawl breaks out between the noble feuding families of Capulet and Montague. Benvolio, a Montague tries to keep the peace but fiery Tybalt, a Capulet, persist until Lords Capulet and Montague can't resist fighting too. Prince Escalus who rules Verona threatens future fighters with execution.

Montague misses his miserable and secretive son Romeo. He asks Benvolio to find the cause of his misery. Romeo reveals he is in love with Rosaline, a Capulet. He wants what he can't have, but she resists his sexual advances and his bribes of gold.

Act 1 Scene 2

Meanwhile, Paris, a rich relative of the Prince, wants to marry Capulet's daughter, Juliet, making the Capulets much more powerful than the Montagues. Capulet tells Paris to wait two years, since Juliet is still thirteen. Capulet himself regrets having married Juliet's mother when she was so young. Capulet organises a masquerade ball and invites Paris to compare Juliet to the other Capulets there.

Act 1 Scene 3

Juliet's mother and the Nurse excitedly explain to her that handsome, rich, posh Paris has made a marriage proposal and is coming to the ball. Juliet agrees to consider him as a suitor.

Act 1 Scene 4

Meanwhile, Romeo and Benvolio intercept Capulet's illiterate servant with invitations to the ball. Benvolio decides they should crash the party as Rosaline will be there, and won't compare to the other beauties Romeo will meet at the masque.

Romeo tells Benvolio and their witty friend Mercutio that he has had a dream of death. The dream suggested attending the Capulet's ball might lead to a terrible fate. But Mercutio mocks Romeo and persuades him to go anyway.

Act 1 Scene 5

Sunday night. Here, he sees Juliet dancing with Paris and instantly forgets about Rosaline. His is in love with Juliet at first sight. Tybalt recognises Romeo's voice (as the party goers are masked) and tells Capulet, hoping he will order Romeo beaten, battered or killed. Capulet enrages Tybalt by telling him to chill. Meanwhile, Romeo and Juliet speak to each other in poetry, sharing the lines of a sonnet their love makes up on the spot. They kiss, not knowing each other's names. The party ends and as Romeo leaves they both discover they are the children of their parents' sworn enemies.

Act 2 Scene 1

Monday morning. Romeo dumps Benvolio and Mercutio.

Act 2 Scene 2 *Balcony scene*

He sneaks back over the high garden walls and stands beneath Juliet's balcony as she speaks to the night about her love for him. They tell each other they are in love. Romeo asks to be satisfied, so Juliet asks him to arrange a marriage. By tomorrow.

Act 2 Scene 3

Romeo rushes to Friar Lawrence, who is the priest both he and Juliet confess to. Romeo asks him to marry them in secret. The Friar thinks this marriage is madness, then flips his thinking, feeling that the lovers' union will unite the feuding families and end the violence in Verona's streets. He agrees to marry them that very afternoon so that they will still be virgins when they wed.

Act 2 Scene 4

Benvolio and Mercutio engage in sexual banter and Romeo suggests he has spent the night away from them because he was having sex. Romeo tells the Nurse of the marriage plans.

Act 2 Scene 5

The Nurse teases Juliet, then tells her to go to Friar Lawrence, to pretend to go to confession, but actually to be married.

Act 2 Scene 6 *— Secret marriage*

Friar Lawrence tells them their marriage is a holy plan, but won't leave them alone till after the wedding in case they start having sex in the church.

Act 3 Scene 1

Meanwhile Tybalt looks to challenge Romeo to a duel following the provocation of his presence at the Capulet ball. He and his Capulet crew find Benvolio and Mercutio and the Montagues. He demands to know where Romeo is, and enrages Mercutio who wants to fight Tybalt himself. Just then, newly married Romeo arrives to hear Tybalt's challenge. Tybalt is now Romeo's cousin because of his secret marriage, so he declines to duel. He tells Tybalt to be satisfied that he loves him. Tybalt assumes this is a taunt, ridiculing his manliness, and demands a duel. Romeo refuses.

Mercutio can't accept Romeo's unmanly submission and makes it his mission to fight Tybalt himself. They duel, but Romeo leaps in, grabbing Mercutio to prevent bloodshed or death. Tybalt stabs Mercutio while he is restrained. Mercutio pretends the stabbing is a scratch, and tells a string of jokes laughing at the wound though he realises he is dying. He curses the Capulets and Montagues with a plague. Then Mercutio dies.

Tybalt returns and Romeo kills him in revenge. He begins to realise his dream of death and fate are coming true and in despair he flees to find the Friar. The Prince, finding Mercutio dead, demands that his killer must be executed. But then he hears Romeo has already terminated Tybalt, so the Prince decides Romeo will be exiled rather than executed. He must leave for Mantua by dawn, never to return to Verona.

Act 3 Scene 2

Juliet is longing for her wedding night and finally consummating the marriage. The Nurse tells her Romeo has killed Tybalt, and reduces her to tears. But she sides with her husband and longs for him to come to her side.

Act 3 Scene 3

Meanwhile, Romeo moans about his misery to the Friar, flinging himself to the floor and weeping because banishment is worse than death. The Friar tells him to grow a pair. He then arranges for Romeo to climb Juliet's balcony to consummate the marriage. The Nurse arrives and she prepares to lead Romeo to his ladder of lovemaking.

Act 3 Scene 4

Monday night. Parish pushes Capulet to let him wed Juliet while she is young. Capulet, distraught at Juliet's tears over Tybalt, thinks a marriage to the perfect partner Paris will soothe her grief. Trying to be the perfect Elizabethan parent, he rushes the wedding for three days' time.

Act 3 Scene 5

Romeo and Juliet consummate the marriage. Romeo leaves for Mantua just after dawn, risking death for a few more stolen minutes with Juliet. They romantically picture each other as corpses as they part.

Tuesday Morning. Lady Capulet tells Juliet of the joyful marriage to Paris. Juliet bursts into tears and refuses. Capulet is astonished at Juliet's refusal. He resorts to threats and tells her he will drag her to the church or chuck her on to the streets to starve if she won't wed on Thursday. Her mother calls her a fool, wishes Juliet were dead and refuses to speak to her.

Juliet turns for advice from the Nurse, who realises her own role in this will jeopardise her job. She cunningly suggests that Juliet should keep Romeo a secret and marry Paris too, pointing out he is both a better man than Romeo and also present.

Act 4 Scene 1

Unfortunately, this bigamous marriage would condemn Juliet's soul to hell, so she seeks solace and advice from the Friar. Paris arrives and tells her that she must love him, because he is the vainest man in Verona. She shoos him away without revealing her marriage to Romeo. She tells the Friar she will kill herself unless he intervenes. Coincidentally, the Friar is a herbalist, and has perfected a poison which perfectly mimics death for forty-two hours. He tells Juliet to drink it tomorrow tonight. She will be found apparently dead and then laid out in the family tomb, rather than buried. In two days' time, the potion will be purged and she will wake ready to be reunited with Romeo, in Mantua. He tells her to apologise to her father and not to be too girly to drink the potion.

Act 4 Scene 2

Juliet apologises and Capulet sends a messenger to tell Paris that the wedding is on for Thursday. Her parents are ecstatic.

Act 4 Scene 3

Tuesday night. Juliet says goodbye to her mother, who suspects nothing. She faces her fears that the Friar might try to poison her with the potion, or she might wake next to her ancestors' corpses and beat out her own brains with their bones. She drinks!

Act 4 Scene 4

Her parents and the Nurse celebrate as they prepare the feast. Lady Capulet tells her husband that he won't be able to have any more affairs, and he is delighted that she still cares.

Act 4 Scene 5

Wednesday morning. The Friar's plan is perfect, and the poison works without killing Juliet. The family are filled with grief. The Friar criticises the Capulets for trying to advance their status through marriage and tell them to be happy that her soul has advanced to heaven, with God.

Paris arrives with musicians playing for the wedding procession. Awkward. Capulet tells Paris that death has taken Juliet's virginity away. Paris is gutted. Peter persuades the poor musicians to sing at the funeral instead.

Friar Lawrence writes to Romeo, outlining his incredible intervention and promising Juliet will soon join him to continue their blissful union.

Act 5 Scene 1

Thursday Morning. The letter never reaches Romeo. Instead, his buddy Balthasar bears the news of Juliet's death to Romeo.

Romeo pays a poor apothecary to sell him a poison powerful enough to kill with a tiny dose.

Act 5 Scene 2

Thursday night. The messenger, Friar John, tells Friar Lawrence that he has been quarantined in a house of plague so the letter to Romeo was not delivered. So Fate, and Mercutio's curse did bring that plague. The Friar sets off to Juliet's tomb.

Act 5 Scene 3

Romeo returns to Verona determined to die at Juliet's side. Poor Paris is strewing flowers outside Juliet's tomb when Romeo and Balthasar arrive with tools to tear open the doors. Romeo gives Balthasar some money and a suicide letter for Montague, his father, to read when Romeo is dead. Paris prevents Romeo breaking in, believing Tybalt's killer wants to desecrate the tomb and interfere with the body of his fiancé. Romeo has had enough of killing, but Paris will not be put off so, reluctantly, Romeo kills him. Paris's dying wish is to be placed near Juliet, so Romeo drags his corpse to her. He finds Juliet, lies down next to her, marvels at her beauty and imagines death must want to be her lover. He drinks his poison, and dies.

Meanwhile the Friar has heard that Romeo did not receive his message and he rushes to the tomb to meet the waking Juliet before Romeo arrives. Unfortunately, he finds Paris dead, and inside, Romeo's dead body next to the waking Juliet. He tells her the bad news, that her husband and future husband are both dead. He hurries her, and tells her of his cunning plan, that she can become a nun. Juliet is having none of this, and refuses to leave. The Friar fears the consequences of his secret part in the tragedy being discovered. He flees, leaving Juliet on her own with Romeo. She decides to die, tries to drink Romeo's poison, but finds none left. She kills herself with Romeo's dagger.

The Watch arrives and Balthasar and the Friar fill in the grieving parents and the Prince. Romeo's mother has already died from grief over Romeo's exile. The Prince pronounces everyone punished, including himself for being too lenient, and losing two kinsmen in Mercutio and Paris.

Capulet and Montague end the feud and promise to commission gold statues of each other's dead children, to celebrate their lives and the ending of the feud.

The Prince turns teacher and tells everyone to talk about what they've learned.

The End

The Prologue

1. It is spoken by the Chorus. In Greek Tragedy, the Chorus was a group of actors, speaking in unison, commenting on the tragedy. In Elizabethan plays the Chorus was a single actor, dressed in black, breaking the fourth wall to remind us that we are watching a construct, to admire the actors and the playwright.

2. The Prologue is written as a Shakespearean sonnet. The sonnet was the most popular form of love poetry. Shakespeare was just as famous for his poetry, and probably wrote love poems for wealthy patrons when the theatres were closed due to plague. *R & J written in 1595*

3. The Prologue gives away the ending of the plot, with the lovers' death, because the story of Romeo and Juliet had been well known for over 100 years, and for the last 30 years from the poem written by Arthur Brooke, *The Tragicall Historye of Romeus and Juliet* (1562). It was the first English translation of that story, and was Shakespeare's main source. The audience wanted to experience Shakespeare's retelling - they wanted to enjoy familiar elements with a new spin.

4. Shakespeare keeps the story in Verona in Italy because it allows the audience to laugh at the behaviour of foreigners, and in particular, Catholics. Catholics were not allowed to worship in England, so a lot of the events of the play don't just explore the human condition, but also the immorality of Catholics. Take a look at Friar Lawrence later to see what I mean.

5. **"From forth the fatal loins of these two foes** *Parents also to be blamed*
    A pair of star-crossed lovers take their life"
    Fate is to be blamed
    The Prologue blames Fate for the lovers' death, which is why they are "star-crossed". Fate is always the cause of tragedy in Greek tragedy. But, the lovers also come "from forth the fatal loins" of their parents. So, this fate is caused by the parents - the audience are asked how far we should blame them. The fricative alliteration is also an expression of disgust from the Chorus, which suggests we should disapprove of the parents. They, and the feud, are most to blame.

Act 1 Scene 1

1. Shakespeare loves starting his plays in mid conversation, so we are sucked into the action and have to work out what has led up to this moment. This is called starting 'in media res'. Here Sampson and Gregory are setting us up for a brawl.
    2 contrasting different things together

2. Shakespeare starts with humour. This juxtaposition with the tragedy keeps the audience guessing. It also helps the audience to enjoy the mockery of Italians and Catholics. We could argue that, until Mercutio is killed, the first half of the play is all comedy. Perhaps this is a lot more like real life. Tragedy hits us when we least expect it, and happiness doesn't last.

3. Sampson and Gregory are actually obsessed with sex. Their whole humour is based on sexual puns. On the one hand this is very funny. On the other hand, it is often brutal. We have to ask how far Shakespeare is asking his audience to criticise this teenage, masculine behaviour. Is he asking the audience to question the culture of patriarchal society? Or is he simply describing the world as it is, and enjoying the humour, even though it is incredibly disrespectful of women?

4. All the humour is based on puns - words with more than one meaning, and on penises. So, Sampson is going to "thrust [Montague's] maids to the wall", meaning to rape them. Then "maids" becomes "maidenhead". Maid meant woman, but maidenhead meant virginity. So now he is boasting that he is just going to rape the virgins. Instead of drawing his sword, Gregory asks him to draw his "tool", which has the double meaning of penis. Sampson picks up on this, and calls it his "naked weapon". You get the idea. But remember, these are also teenagers - the audience might just be invited to laugh at their immaturity and bravado. Or perhaps Shakespeare is saying: 'look, this isn't funny, we live in a society where young men are all armed and dangerous - are they really so different when they become men?' After all, they act on behalf of Capulet and Montague, who join in the fight. Is this a play deliberately commenting on the problems of a patriarchal society?

5. Shakespeare uses a real Italian insult to make fun of them, and of Italians: **"I will bite my thumb at them, which is a disgrace to them, if they bear it."** If the Elizabethan's bit their thumbs as an insult, Sampson wouldn't need to explain this. But the gesture itself looks childish, like sucking a thumb, so it also suggests the feud is childish.

6. The brawl will involve all levels of society, from the Prince, to the Lords Capulet and Montague, to the family servants. Shakespeare wants to show that this kind of feud amongst noble families affects the whole of society. It also works as a symbolic warning of the civil unrest that would come to England if there was any return of Catholicism. This was a particular fear in 1597, when Queen Elizabeth was old (she would die in 1603) and without an heir. The country feared what sort of civil war, or Catholic invasion might happen when she died. Remember, Catholic Spain had tried to invade less than a decade before, in 1588, with the Armada.

7. The opening introduces many of the themes of the play. Masculine honour and the problems of violence in a patriarchal society. The question of Romeo's love and whether it is real - is he really different from the other young men who see women as objects, simply vessels for sex? Gregory and Sampson are Montagues, fantasising about having sex with Capulet women. Romeo is a Montague, fantasising about having sex with Capulet Rosaline. Although Romeo talks of love, is he that different?

8. We only meet Romeo after the fight so that Shakespeare can tease us with the question of how different Romeo is to the sex obsessed Sampson and Gregory.

9. He announces that he is in love. We learn that he is obsessed with sex, and has actually been trying to bribe Rosaline with **"saint seducing gold"** to have sex with him. Rosaline is also a Capulet, so we question whether Romeo is simply acting out a teenage rebellion against his parents. Social structures and courtship rituals made it difficult to meet a woman unchaperoned. To meet a Capulet, his family's enemy, was therefore probably a deliberate act, rather than a chance encounter. To put it bluntly - Romeo is desperate to have sex with a Capulet virgin. How different is he from the bravado of the Capulet servant, Sampson, who wants to rape Montague virgins?

10. Shakespeare wants us to meet Rosaline before Juliet. She is much more mature than Romeo, as he himself implies - his love is "childish" like "Cupid" while she has "Dian's wit" in keeping her chastity. You remember Cupid, the little baby boy with wings and a bow and arrow? Diana was the Roman goddess of hunting and virginity. The comparison invites us to see her as older than Romeo. Shakespeare also asks us to consider how restrictive this social convention. Preserving her

virginity means a woman cannot act on her desires. This will be an interesting contrast to Juliet, who is so desperate to have sex with Romeo that she tells him to arrange a marriage by "tomorrow", the day after they have met. She uses social convention to make sure she can act on her desires.

Act 1, Scene 2

1. One of the ways we can measure social change for women is the average age of marriage. Over the course of the 1500s, the average age went from 21 to 25, whereas in Italy the average age was closer to 20. Shakespeare appears to be ridiculing the Italian tradition of marrying young. This is why we find out Juliet is two weeks away from being 14. He also lets us know that Juliet's mother was already pregnant with Juliet at the same age, and that Capulet believes this may have been a mistake. He tells Paris, **"And too soon marred are those so early made"** into wives. Partly this ridicules Italians. More importantly it deliberately asks the audience to think how far women should have independent lives of their own, and how far their identity should depend on the fathers who control them, and the men they marry.

2. **"But woo her, gentle Paris, get her heart.**
   My will to her consent is but a part.
   An she agreed within her scope of choice,
   Lies my consent and fair according voice."

   Capulet has chosen a stunning match for Juliet. Wealth - check. Good looks - check. Social influence with a family of incredibly high status - check. In the Elizabethan era this was like Meghan Markle being matched to Prince Harry. (Well, the rank of county is equivalent to an Earl, more royal than a Lord). Not only is he the perfect father, he is also what Elizabethans would have thought of as modern, not forcing Juliet into marriage. Instead, she will be able to choose who she marries from a range of suitors. Moreover, though he is unlikely to find a better son in law than Paris, Capulet actually asks him to wait "two more summers" before marrying Juliet. Still though, the best-case scenario is that she will still be 16. Elizabethans would have found this just as shocking as we do. So, perhaps Shakespeare is asking his audience to question how women are treated in a patriarchal society, especially in noble families.

3. Benvolio suggests that Romeo should attend Capulet's ball so that he can compare Rosaline to the "admired beauties of Verona". This is the first step on Romeo's road to tragedy: not love of Juliet, but lust for Rosaline. Romeo will show his hubris by claiming that no women will ever match Rosaline. But Benvolio's hubris starts the tragedy, thinking that gate-crashing the Capulet ball is the solution to Romeo's problems.

4. Romeo's hubris is that he arrogantly believes he can attend Capulet's ball, even though his family is Capulet's greatest enemy. If love had drawn him to the party, we might feel more sympathy for Romeo. But we know it is simple hubris, arrogance which draws him, because we don't believe in Romeo's love. In fact, his reason for going is even worse, he simply wants to win a bet: **"I'll go along, no such sight to be shown, / But to rejoice in splendour of mine own."**

5. What would have happened if the servant could read? He wouldn't have had to show his list of invitations to Romeo, and Romeo would never have entered into the bet with Benvolio. Obviously, the scene is so much more comic if the servant is illiterate. But this is also a cause of the tragedy.

So, at a deeper level, Shakespeare is criticising society. The Capulet's are one of the richest families in Verona, but they see no value in teaching their servants to read. Nor does Veronese society seem to have schools for the children of labouring families. In England, this had changed dramatically. Here, Petty schools were subsidised by the various guilds of merchants, who needed literate and numerate apprentices in their work. Shakespeare went to one. We can see that Shakespeare is contrasting Verona with English society, and making illiteracy a root cause of social tragedy.

Act 1 Scene 3

1. This scene also starts with another comic servant, the Nurse. Shakespeare uses her to create a realistic setting. This is why she links Juliet's birthday to Lammas Tide and a famous earthquake, **"Tis since the earthquake now eleven years".** This cleverly allows Shakespeare to set the play in the heat of summer, which will be important in bringing the heat of the Italian setting to life. Because it is so hot, the characters will behave in a hot-headed way or, in sexual terms, with too much heat or lust. Capulet will be "too hot" when he forces Juliet to marry Paris. Tybalt will kill Mercutio and Romeo will in turn kill Tybalt when "the day is hot". Shakespeare is suggesting that the national climate is partly responsible for the tragedy - in other words, they're Italian, their brains are fried, what else do you expect.

2. The earthquake, however, is very English. It refers to the famous earthquake of 1580 which was strongest at the channel, but still severe in London. This helps Shakespeare make the Italian setting a comment on England. Although he makes fun of the differences between the English and Italians, here he is warning of the similarities. The earthquake is also an ominous portent, a symbolic warning of the destruction that could happen in England if succession is not settled before Queen Elizabeth dies. The Catholics are coming!

3. Shakespeare uses servants throughout the play to comment on social status, what we would call class divisions. First, Shakespeare always makes fun of the servant classes. So, the Nurse is a comic character, and we laugh at her because of her low social status. But next Shakespeare also uses her to criticise the wealthy and the nobility. This is why Juliet's mother insists on her social superiority, dismissing the Nurse so that she can talk to Juliet about her proposed engagement to Paris. Then she immediately realises that her snobbery is misplaced - the Nurse actually has a much better relationship with Juliet, and Lady Capulet needs her to persuade Juliet to think about marriage:

   > **"Nurse, give leave awhile,**
   > **We must talk in secret.—Nurse, come back again.**
   > **I have remembered me. Thou's hear our counsel."**

   But he isn't just saying that Elizabethans should treat their servants better. He is also playing on society's fears. How far should we trust our servants? After all, without the Nurse, there would be no marriage to Romeo. How far can we know our children? Even though Juliet is supervised at all times, Romeo still finds a way to have sex with her.

4. The Nurse remembers Juliet, falling on her face aged two, and the Nurse's husband picking her up and saying, **"Thou wilt fall backward when thou hast more wit, Wilt thou not, Jule?"** The Nurse still finds this hilarious. In this way, Shakespeare is pointing out how women have been

conditioned into accepting their status as sexual objects. Her husband also highlights how enjoyable sex will be for Juliet - she will use her "wit" to get a lover, because sex is worth having. This now works as a foreshadowing of how she takes Romeo as a lover - as you will see, it isn't just Romeo's idea, but Juliet's "wit".

Shakespeare uses the Nurse to point out that girls are bred for sex from birth. We can see this as part of the same male, patriarchal humour belittling women with which he started the play. Again, it is funny. But perhaps Shakespeare is also pointing out that it is part of the characters' tragedy – society finds the terrible things which happen to women funny.

5. Lady Capulet's imagery shows that a woman's sexual attractiveness and virginity are her main ways of acquiring status in society. She points this out to Juliet, with the image of a fish in the sea: **"The fish lives in the sea, and 'tis much pride/ For fair without the fair within to hide."** It is a weird metaphor, where Paris is the fish she must catch, hidden beneath the sea. "Fish" was full of symbolism in Elizabethan England though. First, Catholics were ridiculed as fish-eaters, because they traditionally ate fish on a Friday. So, Shakespeare is making fun of the arranged marriage for such a young daughter as a ridiculous idea. Now the tragedy is that the protagonists live in a Catholic, rather than a Protestant society. Again, Shakespeare is playing on the social fears of Catholic invasion.

But, perhaps more commonly, "fish" is slang both for vagina, and a prostitute. Here, Lady Capulet is also asking Juliet to sell her virginity to the highest bidder. Shakespeare is pointing out that the rules of patriarchal society treat the daughters of the nobility as prostitutes, trading them for sex. Lady Capulet has also been conditioned to accept this, and so she points out the financial benefits. Paris is a golden book **"That in gold clasps locks in the golden story."** She is emphasising the wealth Juliet will receive, repeating "gold". But the other part of the image is that her story will be locked inside Paris's book - it is an image which portrays women as trapped. Wealthy women are simply trapped in a golden cage. They are not able to write their own stories, but are always trapped inside a man's.

Act 1 Scene 4

1. Mercutio gets his name from mercurial, to mean witty, intelligent and unpredictable. It also derives from Mercury, the Roman messenger god. The first describes Mercutio's personality, but the second describes his function in the play - he carries important messages, perhaps to help us understand Shakespeare's point of view. Mercutio is incredibly cynical about love, and believes men are simply motivated by sexual desire.

2. This scene, and Mercutio's famous Queen Mab speech, is about dreams. On the one hand he recreates a character from English folk lore - the queen of the fairies, "fairies' midwife". Her name changes in *A Midsummer Night's Dream* to Titania. These stories appear innocent, and would have been familiar to his audience from stories they heard as children. But on the other hand, Shakespeare also uses Mercutio to point out that dreams reveal our darkest desires.

3. Mercutio's famous Queen Mab speech is a cynical attack on dreams and our unspoken desires. Queen Mab invades people's dreams and simply gives them more of what they want, so that their desires seem corrupt. So, courtiers at court dream of "curtsies", finding a rich wife at court.

Lawyers don't dream of justice, but "fees". Women don't dream of love, but "kisses" and are so promiscuous that they contract sexually transmitted disease which, without antibiotics, "blisters" them. Rather than saving people's souls, or improving the lives of the poor, the Parson dreams of more money, "another benefice". Rather than defending his country, the soldier dreams of "cutting foreign throats" just because they are foreign and therefore Catholic.

This corruption builds to a climax, where Queen Mab makes young women dream, not just of sex, but having children, **"That presses them and learns them first to bear". He likens this to "much misfortune".** So, Mercutio's final point is that the worst tragedy of society is that women are forced to have children. Elizabethan women knew this often led to their own deaths, and the deaths of their children. We remember Juliet is now an only child as her siblings have all been "swallowed up" and the Nurse's daughter Susan has also died young. Mercutio is therefore attacking the patriarchal control of women, forcing them into childbirth. It suggests patriarchal control is going to be a significant cause of Juliet's tragedy.

Finally, he links this dreaming to "Quean" and "Mab". Both these words were Elizabethan slang for "whore". He's suggesting that all our dreams are corrupt, they all involve exploiting others but that the worst exploitation is the way society exploits women.

4. This scene reveals Mercutio is carried away with fun, with verbal puns and imagination, but also that this humour is excessive. Both Benvolio and Romeo have to stop him talking, and his imagery is always violent and sexual. Perhaps this is also part of his role as messenger. He's telling us that the main cause of the tragedy is the way this patriarchal society controls women, using them for breeding and for sexual pleasure. The only male character who seems genuinely to want to avoid violence at all costs is Benvolio.

5. Romeo's hubris is also emphasised through his dream:

> **"my mind misgives**
> **Some consequence yet hanging in the stars**
> **Shall bitterly begin his fearful date**
> **With this night's revels".**

The references to "consequence" and "stars" reveal that this is a dream about his fate. His fate will "begin" if he goes to the ball, to the "revels". His hubris is that he goes anyway, believing he can outwit fate. There is also another possibility. Mercutio has revealed that our dreams reveal what we really want. This invites us to ask if Romeo's tragedy isn't falling in love with Juliet, but that he actually desires a tragic fate, a tragic death. This will explain why he seeks out Rosaline, a Capulet, and why he will fall in love with another Capulet, Juliet. He isn't just trying to rebel against his parents, he is also attracted to self-destruction. He ends the scene by giving up his sense of self: **"But he that hath the steerage of my course, Direct my sail."** He is going to act without worrying about the consequences.

Act 1 Scene 5

1. Ok, you run a patriarchal society, in which your rich daughter needs to attract a husband from a family at least as noble, wealthy and politically well-connected as your own. How will she attract such a husband? Daughters would learn what was fashionable, probably, embroidery, music,

singing, and dance. Virtually the only social contexts in which Juliet might meet a man are chaperoned and orchestrated. Compare this to the young men of Verona who roam freely, while girls and young women are permanently supervised. This means that a dance is a big deal. Now, why a masqued ball? It provides anonymity, at least in theory. The illusion of secrecy allows for the secret sharing of information or feelings. You also react to a person of the opposite sex on a more physical level - you focus on their body, and how they dance and move, and the quality and rhythm of their voice. The dances too are all choreographed. Everyone knows the steps, knows when to swap partners, knows when to touch, which allows conversation and flirtation, and you know which dances involve athleticism or physical display. The masks are essential as a plot device, so that Romeo can enter without being recognised. But it doesn't just exist in the world of the play - it is designed to help young men and women become attracted to each other in Elizabethan society.

2. This is exactly what happens to Romeo:

> **"Oh, she doth teach the torches to burn bright!**
> **It seems she hangs upon the cheek of night**
> **Like a rich jewel in an Ethiope's ear,**
> **Beauty too rich for use, for earth too dear.**
> **So shows a snowy dove trooping with crows**
> **As yonder lady o'er her fellows shows.**
> **The measure done, I'll watch her place of stand,**
> **And, touching hers, make blessèd my rude hand."**

He has watched her dance the "measure" and compared her movements to the "trooping" of "crows" who are inferior to her. Juliet is contrasted as a superior "snowy dove". So, it is a physical reaction to her body and the way it moves. You might also notice that he picks up on the metaphor Benvolio introduced when he told Romeo he would show him women that made Rosaline, his "swan" look like "a crow". Perhaps the shift from "swan" to "dove" reveals that this attraction is based on love, as the dove is a symbol of love. But watch out for Mercutio's comments later, which show that this rhyme of "dove" and "love" is just lazy poetry. Mercutio the messenger is telling us that this love is not real.

3. Shakespeare loves to play with irony. Tybalt is hot-headed, and wants to challenge Romeo to a duel for daring to mock the Capulets by attending the ball. His family honour has been challenged, and his moral code demands that he makes Romeo pay. After all, this is what the "ancient grudge" demands. He tells Capulet **"Now, by the stock and honour of my kin/ To strike him dead I hold it not a sin."** But the irony is that Capulet notices and forbids Tybalt from acting. Crucially, he does not have Romeo ejected. If only he had listened to Tybalt, he could have saved the life of his daughter. Ironically, by trying to stop violence in his "house" he causes a violent end to his house (as Juliet is his only living child). Just to make us appreciate the irony, this happens exactly before Romeo and Juliet meet. The other irony is that this moment turns Tybalt from a duellist desperate to fight any Montague, to one determined to kill only one: Romeo.

4. Romeo begins with the first quatrain of a sonnet. Juliet replies with a quatrain of her own, perfectly continuing the rhyme scheme of his sonnet. This immediately signals to the audience that, though the love is at first sight, it is real. They are suited to each other - completing each other's lines.

5. But the sonnet is full of surprises. The original form of sonnet is Italian, from the poet Petrarch. In a Petrarchan sonnet, the twist, or surprise is called the Volta. The Volta always occurs directly after line eight - the last line of the octave. The sonnet is always divided into two parts. The final part is six lines, and so is called the sestet. The first line of the sestet introduces the turn, the Volta. So, Shakespeare pitches an Italian love poem in his Italian love story. Wait. There's more. Shakespeare preferred a more dramatic Volta, and in all Shakespearian sonnets the Volta happens in the final couplet. This makes the switch more sudden. The genius of this sonnet is that Romeo has planned his seduction with a Petrarchan Volta at line 9. But the sudden twist at line 11 has been better planned by Juliet. This fits with the source poem, in Juliet frequently has to take the lead.

6. To understand the first Volta, we have to appreciate Romeo's clever, but sacrilegious religious imagery. He calls Juliet a "shrine" and offers to kiss the hand he pretends to have offended with his "rough touch". He knows he wants to kiss her hand and, from there, will see if he can come up with a clever way to encourage Juliet to kiss him. Juliet pretends to reject him, by declining the kiss. As a woman, she mustn't appear in any way sexually available. But she is already, apparently, falling in love with him, so she wants to kiss him, just as much as he wants to kiss her.

   So, she changes his imagery so that she is not a "shrine", but the statue of a "saint" in church. This allows her to show how saints hands kiss "palm to palm". To do this, however, she must take hold of his hands, **"For saints have hands that pilgrims' hands do touch"**. In appearing to reject him, she has doubled the physical contact to both hands. Clever! She has also changed his "hand" to "palm", and then "palm" to "palmer". A palmer was a term for a pilgrim returning from the Holy Land. One of the souvenirs they would all bring back was a cross made out of palm tree leaves. The use of this religious imagery is clever, funny - because physical seduction is not what the Bible has in mind - and also shockingly transgressive. She is daring him to follow her lead: she will reject the "palm" but wants Romeo to find a way to get her to accept the whole "palmer" - all of himself.

   Romeo follows. So now comes Romeo's Volta, as he seizes his chance to suggest they kiss: **"O, then, dear saint, let lips do what hands do."** Social conventions of modesty prevent Juliet from taking the initiative here by kissing him, but we can see that she has led the conversation to make it easier for him to kiss her. Next, she tells him that, as a saint, she expects to be kissed by the pilgrim, to "grant" the pilgrim's prayer. This is the final Volta - he began just trying to kiss her hand, and she has engineered the conversation to make sure that he kisses her lips: **"Saints do not move, though grant for prayers' sake."**

7. The religious imagery has two competing and opposite functions. The religious purity suggests that their love is real, and pure, and will carry God's blessing. Conversely, it is almost blasphemous, being used as a cover for the lovers to explore their sexual desire. Which way is Shakespeare pushing us? Well, King Henry VIII, Elizabeth's father, effectively outlawed the Catholic faith. Monasteries and convents were destroyed. Worshipping saints and their statues was seen as idolatrous - the statues were idols, false gods, and so they were stripped out of English churches. Knowing this, we can see that the religious imagery of saints suggests the love is wrong headed, a false faith, just as Catholicism is a false faith in England.

8. Remember this is the second sonnet of the play, with the first being the prologue which laid out the tragedy. By having the lovers share the lines of a sonnet as they share their first kiss, Shakespeare is also suggesting this is the moment which seals their tragic fate. This would suggest they are punished for their blasphemous use of religious imagery. We will be reminded of that in

the next scene when Juliet calls Romeo "god of her idolatry". This is a direct challenge to god, a classic example of hubris. It suggests that in worshipping each other above God they deserve to be punished.

9. Juliet's reaction to Romeo's second kiss is **"You kiss by the book".** One interpretation you'll often hear is that she is making fun of him, because he kisses like someone who has only read about it in books. But this seems unlikely, given that it is the moment they fall in love. So, the more logical possibility is that Juliet means it as praise - Romeo kisses so well that it is as though he has learned the instruction manual on kissing - in other words, he has had lots of practice. This might be relative of course. We don't know how much older Romeo is than Juliet, but he will certainly have more experience of kissing than her. The Friar tells Romeo that his love for Rosaline was not real: **"Oh, she knew well, / Thy love did read by rote that could not spell."** This metaphor suggests that Romeo has only been playing at love. So, we might infer that, though Juliet is delighted and enraptured by Romeo, it may not be because their love is real. It could simply be that they are both too young to understand their feelings, or to view them with a more mature perspective.

We are given a strong hint that Juliet is immature in her reaction to Romeo, telling the Nurse **"If he be married. My grave is like to be my wedding bed."** She expects men to be unfaithful, but will remain faithful to him even if he is married. It is very possible that the Nurse takes this to mean that she will become his mistress, rather than get married. The metaphor also ironically sums up her fate - when Romeo is married, her wedding bed does become a her grave.

10.   The Nurse also gives us an interesting interpretation of noble marriages. She tells Romeo of Juliet, **"I tell you, he that can lay hold of her/ Shall have the chinks."** Here the husband offers up his family reputation, wealth and political influence. In return, the husband receives a beautiful, young bride, but also a dowry - "the chinks" - even more wealth. This presents marriage as a financial exchange. Shakespeare juxtaposes this with the lovers' perspective, to ask whether their immature love is much better than the adult alternative.

Act 2 Scene 1 and Prologue

1. The second Chorus gives us authorial viewpoint and social commentary. The Chorus tells us that Juliet "as much in love, her means much less/ To meet her new beloved anywhere." This seems to criticise the unequal freedoms young men have compared to young women. It is also a statement of fact: she is "much in love". Shakespeare is inviting us to see Juliet's love as real, rather than too sudden and too young. He's also pointing out how constrained a daughter's life is. He appears deeply critical of this kind of restrictive society, calling the restrictions placed on women "extremities" in **"Tempering extremities with extreme sweet."** The "sweet" of their love is portrayed as a reaction to the "extremities" placed on women. This causes their love to become "extreme" in its sweetness. The imagery foreshadows the Friar's later warning before they marry:

> **"The sweetest honey**
> **Is loathsome in his own deliciousness,**
> **And in the taste confounds the appetite.**
> **Therefore love moderately; long love doth so."**

The Chorus implies this excess is not the fault of the lovers' youth, but the fault of the social restriction imposed on women by a patriarchal society. To sum up, because society is extreme in the way women are restricted, women might react in extreme ways.

2. But Mercutio the messenger also acts as a Chorus, commenting on Romeo's love. To him, Romeo's love is a pose. Love poetry typically focused on women who were unattainable, just like Romeo's obsession with Rosaline. The lover would then write poems complaining of his unrequited love. Mercutio mocks Romeo, **"Speak but one rhyme, and I am satisfied. Cry but "Ay me!" Pronounce but "love" and "dove.""** Shakespeare wants this accusation to feel plausible, so he chooses the very word Romeo used to describe Juliet, comparing her to a "dove" among "crows". Ouch - busted.

3. But in the next breath, Mercutio refers to a popular ballad (song) in London, which told the story of love at first sight. The African king Cophetua has no interest in women until he sees a beggar and falls in love her. He stakes his life on marrying her - either he succeeds, or he will commit suicide. They marry, become a beloved king and queen and lead a happy and wonderful life. Mercutio uses the reference to mock Romeo's desire to fall in love.

   Shakespeare uses it ironically - Romeo will marry after love at first sight, but the act of marriage will lead directly to his suicide. Shakespeare included this ballad in four of his plays, suggesting that the song was both a personal and public obsession.

4. Mercutio doesn't believe in love and sees it only as an illusion created by the desire to have sex. He mocks the rules of love poetry, which prescribed the order in which you would describe your lover's face:

   > **"I conjure thee by Rosaline's bright eyes,**
   > **By her high forehead and her scarlet lip,**
   > **By her fine foot, straight leg, and quivering thigh,**
   > **And the demesnes that there adjacent lie"**

But he ends his description showing what Romeo's obsession really is - the area ("demesnes") next to ("adjacent" to) her "quivering thigh". He makes fun of what he sees as Romeo's obsession with sex, and at the same time reveals his own. He imagines Romeo wishing **"his mistress were that kind of fruit / As maids call medlars"**. The medlar, due to the hole in its centre, looked like an "open arse". Mercutio suggests that women call other women who have sex this way - as there is zero risk of pregnancy - "medlar fruit". He then imagines Romeo as another fruit, a "poperin pear" which worked as a symbol for penis - it was an elongated pear, apparently first grown in Poperinge in Belgium. The name caught on in English because it would sound like pop-her-in. Mercutio is pointing out that Romeo is typical of all men, and that all men are simply interested in sex, not love. Using the imagery of fruit also suggests this is simple biology, how nature has made us. After all fruit is how fruit trees reproduce. To dress this biological obsession with sex into an obsession with love is simply an illusion, in Mercutio's view.

5. When we consider Mercutio's imagery we need to match it to his Queen Mab speech. Here, he personified dreams as a whore, and the crescendo of his speech ended with an attack on Queen Mab as a "hag" who forces women to get pregnant through sexual pleasure. One interpretation is that he has a kind of feminist view, ridiculing all men for their sexual obsession. He contrasts this

with the terrible consequences for women, through childbirth. His reference to "medlar fruit" points out the only sensible solution for women is to put men's pleasure ahead of their own, but avoid pregnancy through anal sex.

There are a dizzying number of layers here though. Another possibility is that Mercutio's imagery reveals a disgust at the idea of women having sex, and that he is actually voicing his own homosexual desire for Romeo. After all, if Romeo is dreaming of anal sex, then why confine himself to Rosaline? His observation, **"If love be blind, love cannot hit the mark"** might suggest that Romeo is blind to Mercutio's love for him: Mercutio should be his "mark", his target.

Or it might suggest that Romeo's attraction to the "open arse" is actually an attraction to men. He is suggesting that Romeo doesn't realise he actually wants to have sex with men. This might explain why he pursues women who are likely to reject him, like Rosaline and Juliet, both Capulets.

This offers a tantalising possibility, that Romeo falls in love with Juliet because she still looks like a boy. Remember, he fell in love with her before he saw her face. At thirteen, her body is unlikely to look quite like a woman's. This possibility is even more likely when we consider that all female characters were played by men, and Juliet would have been played by a young teenage male. On the Elizabethan stage Mercutio's imagery plays very deliberately with this tradition, and asks us to consider if Mercutio is actually in love with Romeo.

The other possibility of course is that Mercutio simply means that love is "blind" to its own true nature - it is simply sexual desire.

Act 2 Scene 2

1. It is usual to view Romeo's description of Juliet as deeply poetic, and proof of his love. These lines are probably the most famous from the play:

> **"But soft! What light through yonder window breaks?**
> **It is the east, and Juliet is the sun.**
> **Arise, fair sun, and kill the envious moon"**

We can argue that Juliet has totally transformed Romeo's world, just like the "sun" would if it came out at night. Romeo's imagery perfectly expresses this transformation.

But let me offer an alternative view. These lines come straight after Shakespeare has made Mercutio ridicule Romeo's poetry. The "sun" is also an odd image for a woman. First, it sounds masculine, as a homophone for 'son'. Secondly, the "moon" is symbolic of women. Like women, the moon has a monthly cycle. Romeo himself compared Rosaline to Diana, who was also the goddess of the moon. So, moon would be a logical choice. He has picked on the image of "the sun" because he is thinking about Juliet as superior to Rosaline, but it is an odd fit. Shakespeare makes fun of this imagery in one of his most famous sonnets (130), which begins:

> **"My mistress' eyes are nothing like the sun;**
> **Coral is far more red than her lips' red;"**

In other words, Romeo's poetry here is, as the Friar suggests, learned by "rote" and actually ridiculous. Or not. Shakespeare constantly provokes us to ask how real Romeo's love is, and never tells us what to think.

2. Juliet's poetry is totally different to Romeo:

> **"What's in a name? That which we call a rose**
> **By any other name would smell as sweet;"**

Where he uses imagery as a way to describe Juliet in a poetic way, she uses imagery to problem solve. Romeo is a "rose" because she is intoxicated by his smell, and she points out that the rose is not attractive because it is called a "rose", but because of its nature.

This metaphor is just as odd as Romeo comparing her to the "sun", because a rose would normally symbolise femininity. They have both switched genders in their choice of metaphor. (You will notice that Romeo accuses Juliet's love of making him "effeminate" just before he kills Tybalt).

Juliet contrasts the "rose" deliberately with a list of his body parts, and then coyly refuses to name the one she is thinking about: **"nor any other part / Belonging to a man"**. We know the part she means, the part that only men have. Her problem is in how to marry him so that he can "take all myself".

If she were only thinking about having sex with Romeo, as with any lover, she would have to keep the relationship secret from her parents. The status of their family depends on her staying a virgin.

So, whether her lover is a Montague or not would be beside the point. His name only matters because she wants to marry him.

3. From Juliet's perspective, the whole scene is about problem solving. She has to remind Romeo three times that his life is in danger, "the place death" if he is seen. She knows that he has heard her say she loves him, when she should have followed the conventions of flirting: **"I should have been more strange"** and "coying". This puts her at a disadvantage - he knows her honest feelings, whereas she has to guess at his. Because Romeo speaks like a lover who is simply playing at love, she needs him to "pronounce it faithfully". Her next problem is manoeuvring him into marriage. So, she rejects his poetic desire to swear "by the moon" and then rejects the idea of swearing, "Do not swear at all." She is telling Romeo that promises are not enough and not to be trusted. Now her language changes:

> **"I have no joy of this contract tonight.**
> **It is too rash, too unadvised, too sudden".**

Yes, she appears to be warning Romeo about moving too quickly. But, at the end of the scene she will rush him to come "tomorrow" with news of when they are going to be married. So, she actually has no intention of moving slowly. What she is really interested in is a "contract". This is much more binding than a promise.

4. The next problem is how to get him to propose. They've already kissed (it was her idea - remember the Shakespearian Volta in their sonnet). Remember how she said she should have been "strange" and practised "coyness"? Well, that's what she does now. Her actions say, 'Fine, you say you love me. You know I love you. Goodnight, I'm off to bed'. She says: **"Good night, good night! As sweet repose and rest"**. This has an instant impact on Romeo. Juliet herself has reminded him three times that he is risking his life by being there, so from his point of view, she owes him - and he doesn't even get another kiss.

5. He can't believe what's happening. He protests, **"O, wilt thou leave me so unsatisfied?"** Shakespeare is playing with us again. Does he mean he is "unsatisfied" as they have not discussed a marriage contract, or does he mean he is "unsatisfied" because he is still full of sexual desire? This is exactly what Juliet has been trying to provoke, so she asks him, **"What satisfaction canst thou have tonight?"** In other words, she forces him to consider the marriage "contract" if he wants to have sex with her. Although she believes in love at first sight, she also knows her only way of achieving any kind of status and independence is through marriage. So, she is very, very specific in what Romeo must do:

> **"Thy purpose marriage, send me word tomorrow**
> **By one that I'll procure to come to thee**
> **Where and what time thou wilt perform the rite,**
> **And all my fortunes at thy foot I'll lay**
> **And follow thee my lord throughout the world."**

Romeo has to arrange the marriage by "tomorrow" and know "where and what time" it will happen. In exchange he will have "all my [Juliet's] fortunes". This is not just her love, but her literal fortunes, "the chinks" the Nurse mentioned. In other words, she is reminding Romeo just what she is worth, and why he should hurry. We have to ask how much of this haste is because she is in love, how much is because she doesn't trust Romeo to change his mind, and how much is because she suspects her parents will arrange the marriage to Paris quickly. After all, *we* know Capulet wants Paris to wait two years, but Lady Capulet and the Nurse didn't tell Juliet that. Looked at from this perspective, the tragedy begins with their marriage. So, one possibility is that the cause of the tragedy is the patriarchal exchange, where fathers trade their daughters for wealth and status.

6. Shakespeare plays with us again when Romeo describes his feelings as he moves to leave Juliet:

> **"Love goes toward love as schoolboys from their books,**
> **But love from love, toward school with heavy looks."**

These childlike references deliberately highlight how young both lovers are. They also imply that love has arrived too soon, while they are still learning. So, their youth is also a factor in their tragedy.

7. Juliet introduces the image of falconry. She imagines Romeo as her falcon, and wants to call him back to sit on her glove, **"To lure this tassel-gentle back again"**. This imagery of luring and controlling reveals how she sees that she has controlled him up to now.

Romeo returns to this image when he returns to her, calling her **"my nyas"**, which is a falcon still in its nest, unable to fly. So he also sees himself as in control of her. Juliet recognises Romeo's freedom, literally to roam anywhere in Verona's streets. As a man, patriarchal society is metaphorically somewhere he can fly and hunt.

In contrast, Juliet is still earthbound, unable to fly. In a patriarchal society, this is because she is a woman, or a girl. The shared imagery of falconry perhaps shows that they are well matched. However, each one sees themselves as the falconer. Each one thinks that they are in control of the other. Which one is right? Or, if they are both the falconers, who controls them? Fate? The family feud? Love? Sexual desire? The patriarchal rules restraining women? Their own hubris, arrogantly challenging social convention?

Act 2 Scene 3

1. Shakespeare needs to let us know that the Friar is a herbalist, an expert in the medicinal uses of plants and flowers. This is crucial exposition for when he offers Juliet a drug which mimics death. The Friar tells us all this himself - we get the sense that he is rehearsing a lesson while filling a basket with samples to use. The lesson is about balance, and how all things can be used for good or evil, such as his herbs.

> "For naught so vile that on the earth doth live
> But to the earth some special good doth give;"

He also speaks in rhyming couplets, as though carefully crafting what he wants to say. When Romeo enters, he simply carries on, which implies he had an audience of students in his mind all along. Talking to himself also gives us a sense of madness or eccentricity, which is necessary to help us understand why he would take the risk of marrying Romeo to Juliet. And of course, remember he is a Catholic, and therefore wrong-headed.

2. The Friar already knows all about Romeo's love of Rosaline. This is a stark contrast to his relationship with his own father, who has to ask Benvolio to find out anything about Romeo's mood or whereabouts. This helps us understand how the Friar feels connected to the young people who confess to him - both Romeo and Juliet.

3. Romeo tells how he is in love with Juliet, **"the fair daughter of rich Capulet"**. The added and unnecessary adjective "rich" (because everyone knows who Capulet is) implies that it isn't just love which makes him want to marry Juliet. The "chinks"!

4. The Friar mocks Romeo's former love for Rosaline, **"what a deal of brine / Hath washed thy sallow cheeks for Rosaline!"** This description of Romeo constantly in tears reveals that he is both childish and unmanly. To an Elizabethan audience, Romeo's recent past is ridiculous.

5. Again, Shakespeare is constantly challenging us to decide if Romeo's love is genuine. The Friar certainly doesn't think so. He believes that Romeo is simply feeling lust: **"Young men's love then lies / Not truly in their hearts, but in their eyes."**

6. Romeo tells the Friar that his love for Juliet is different, simply because she loves him in return, and does "love for love allow." Again, not a strong vote for this being genuine love. He's just overjoyed that she has accepted him.

7. The Friar's reaction needs us to understand iambic pentameter. When he says **"Oh, *she* knew well / Thy love did read by rote, that could not spell"**, the iamb tells us the emphasis must be on "she". This means the Friar is contrasting what Rosaline "knew" to Juliet's ignorance. Remember, the Friar knows Juliet well, and he thinks she won't see that Romeo's love is childish and unreal, "learned by rote" rather than experienced. These are some huge hints that Shakespeare thinks their love is too childish to be real.

8. But in the very next line, the Friar makes an unexpected leap. Just as he has finished explaining why both Romeo and Juliet are both too immature to know real love, he decides that he will marry them, **"For this alliance may so happy prove / To turn your households' rancour to pure love"**. Although he doesn't believe in Romeo and Juliet's love, he does believe that the marriage contract, the "alliance", might turn into "pure love" by ending the feud. This reminds us of his view of himself, doing "some special good" even with things which are "vile". Perhaps he doesn't see the love as "vile", but simply immature and misguided.

9. On the other hand, we might want to argue that he also believes in their love, and that this great love is what will persuade the parents to end their quarrel. But unfortunately, this doesn't fit what he has just said about Romeo's love. He doesn't believe him. He calls him "young waverer", and then says that he will only support Romeo "in one respect". This strongly suggests that he believes in the power of the marriage, not of their love.

10.   The suddenness of his decision, especially as it contradicts everything he has previously said, makes his decision seem rash and a dangerous gamble. This makes his final words comically ironic, when he advises Romeo to slow down: **"Wisely and slow. They stumble that run fast."** Clearly,

he should be following his own advice. This again is hubris, arrogantly believing that he can end the feud with his deceit and flouting of social rules.

Act 2 Scenes 4

1. Benvolio and Mercutio are discussing Romeo. Mercutio mocks Romeo's love, claiming Romeo's heart has been **"cleft with the blind bow-boy's butt shaft"**. The alliteration emphasises the "butt". He means that Cupid has managed to pierce Romeo's heart with the blunt end of his arrow. This symbolises how this love is not real, that any woman can make Romeo fall in love with her. The "shaft" is the length of the arrow, and the end which sits on the bowstring is grooved. This is called the "butt" because it is the end, but also because the groove makes it look like buttocks. "Shaft" is also slang for penis. At the very least, Mercutio is again pointing out that Romeo is feeling only lust. But the juxtaposition of imagery describing buttocks and penis is a recurring theme for Mercutio, and it also implies his own sexual desires for Romeo.

2. Mercutio calls Tybalt **"More than Prince of Cats"**. This refers to a character Tibert/Tybalt in medieval stories. Their main character is cunning Reynard, a fox, who outwits the other animals. Perhaps he means that Tybalt will always be outwitted, just as the cat is always outwitted by Reynard. Again, this will be hubris, as Tybalt is going to kill him.

3. He further insults Tybalt by describing the way he fences. Instead of learning to fight, he simply "keep's time", like a dancer. All the fencing moves have Italian names, **"the immortal passado, the punto reverso"** which to Mercutio makes them simply fashionable and ridiculous, rather than of any use in an actual fight.

4. Just as he thinks Romeo's identity as a lover is a youthful pose, so he sees Tybalt's love of fencing as a pose. He is not a fighter, but "a duellist", **"the very butcher of a silk button".** He implies this is all for show, and that Tybalt would not know how to inflict a real wound. This of course is hubris, again.

   Another sign of his hubris is that he has lost control of his iambic pentameter now, and speaks in prose. Shakespeare could be hinting that he has lost control of himself. This implies that the coming duel with Tybalt is highly risky, that perhaps Mercutio's assessment of Tybalt's threat is wrong. It also implies that, in defending male honour, Shakespeare believes he is actually losing status as a human being. This is why he is not allowed to speak in verse.

5. Mercutio describes Romeo in a sexualised way, with the return of "fish" imagery to suggest that Romeo did not go home because he was with a prostitute, "French slop". We expect this from Mercutio, and "slop" also suggests disgust at the thought of Romeo having sex with a woman, rather than with a man.

6. What we call banter, Elizabethan's would have called wordplay. Because they are young men, the wordplay is all about sex. Romeo claims "Why, then is my pump well flowered", where "pump" represents his penis and "flower" represents female genitalia or virginity.

   Mercutio would happily believe he has been with a prostitute, but Romeo's words imply he has finally had sex with the virgin Rosaline. So Mercutio counters that he doesn't believe Romeo. He implies instead that Romeo has been alone with his "pump", wearing it out on his own: **"thou hast**

worn out thy pump, that when the single sole of it is worn...after the wearing solely singular".
"Sole" is a pun because a "pump" is also the name of a light shoe. But what Mercutio is hinting at is that the only sexual pleasure he has had is masturbation.

Remember, the play started with this sexualised wordplay. Shakespeare appears critical of it. Sure, it's funny. But Romeo has just arranged to marry Juliet. Friar Lawrence has just been talking to him about "pure love". And here he is, pretending to be a player. On the one hand, it makes him seem immature. On the other hand, Shakespeare is also asking, is Romeo's marriage to Juliet really about love in his own mind, or is it more the excitement of sex and status?

7. The point of a pun is that it means two things at the same time. Shakespeare uses this as a way of looking at the world - he is constantly challenging us. So, is it real love? What is the real cause of the tragedy? Here Romeo and Mercutio compare their duelling of wits to a "goose chase". Chasing the goose was, on the one hand, a particular kind of follow-my-leader horse race, where the person in the lead got to choose the route. What fun the rich boys had! On the other hand, it refers to chasing sex, where "goose" was slang for a prostitute. Why are the puns all about sex? Well, they suggest that this is all Mercutio can think about. But perhaps that is also true of Romeo.

8. Now Mercutio pretends to lose the battle of wits, claiming he has lost the horse race, as Romeo has **"more of the wild-goose in one of thy wits than, I am sure, I have in my whole five."** (Here he means the five senses). But, if we take the other meaning, he is suggesting that Romeo has more than five times the desire to have sex with the "goose", a woman, than he has. It is close to a confession to Romeo that Mercutio is sexually attracted to him.

9. When the Nurse arrives, she is mocked by Benvolio and Mercutio. Because she is a servant, they feel they can treat her as a figure of fun. Mercutio mocks Romeo that she is the "bawd" or madam of the brothel he spent the night at. Romeo does not react, so he switches tack: **"Romeo, will you come to your father's?"** He has chosen to dine there because he knows Tybalt's letter is waiting, and he wants Romeo to respond to the duel. By placing this after the immature word play around sex, Shakespeare also asks us to view the duel as immature. The whole idea of male and family honour being settled by violence appears ridiculous.

10.   Shakespeare doesn't ask us to have any sympathy with the Nurse, who doesn't seem to understand the sexual insults which come her way. Perhaps this is because she plays a guilty part in the tragedy. Romeo can't marry Juliet unless the Nurse helps him. He also can't consummate the marriage, unless she takes a rope ladder from one of his servants, so that he can climb on to Juliet's balcony. (I love Baz Luhrmann's film, but he shows Leonardo Di Caprio climbing up to Clare Dane's balcony when they *first* meet. That doesn't happen in the play!)

In her defence, the Nurse does try to protect Juliet, by telling Romeo not to **"lead her into a fool's paradise"** because she is so "young". On the other hand, this warning applies equally to the Nurse. She is old enough to realise that Juliet is too young to make the decision to marry. But much worse than this, the idea that this secret marriage can survive the feud is also "a fool's paradise".

Act 2 Scene 5

1. The scene opens with Juliet desperate for news about Romeo from the Nurse. The Nurse delays telling her, teasing her, insisting that Juliet massages her back. The delayed gratification is

amusing, but also keeps Juliet alive - her tragedy is deferred. This makes the scene bitter-sweet. We want her to have news of Romeo, even though we know this will lead to her death.

2. The Nurse is most looking forward to Juliet consummating the marriage, so she talks about sex. But her description of Juliet's first sexual experience, **"But you shall bear the burden soon at night"** is also prophetic. It foreshadows her death - this will be the "burden" that happens because of tonight. On a different level, she is also pointing out that marriage is a "burden" and soon enough she will have to bear children of her own.

Act 2 Scene 6

1. Romeo's happiness at the marriage is ironic. He tells Friar Lawrence, **"Then love-devouring death do what he dare; It is enough I may but call her mine."** This again is hubris, arrogantly daring death to come and kill his love. And it will.

2. The Friar also foreshadows their tragic deaths: **"These violent delights have violent ends"**. He means it as a warning to Romeo not to have such strong emotions. He means that Romeo is deliberately thrill seeking, looking for dangerous experiences in love, such as secretly marrying the daughter of his father's enemy. And through dramatic irony we know death is coming.

3. Even though he is about to marry them, the Friar observes that love is a fantasy, as though he is warning them about going through with the marriage:

   "A lover may bestride the gossamers
   That idles in the wanton summer air,
   And yet not fall. So light is vanity."

4. This imagery of lovers walking on spider webs strongly reminds us of the fairy world of Mercutio's Queen Mab speech. It suggests that their vision of marriage is simply a foolish dream, an impossibility, like walking on a web. However, we remember that what prompted the speech was Romeo's own dream of death if he should attend the ball. The Friar's imagery has the same warning of failure.

5. "Vanity" here means excessive pride. This pride of course is hubris. But the shock is that the Friar is prepared to go through with the marriage, even though he can see their love is such a mistake.

6. He contrasts this "vanity" with the idea of falling. The "fall" is always symbolic of the Fall, the name given to Adam and Eve's falling out of God's favour. This happened in Eden when they rebelled against his instruction not to eat the fruit from the Tree of Knowledge of Good and Evil. Because he does not spell this out, we can infer that this is an unconscious thought. He's linking the marriage to the idea of Original Sin, and so perhaps unconsciously realises his own part in it is wrong.

7. Romeo's first meeting with the Friar was quite different. Then the Friar spoke entirely in rhyming couplets. The world made perfect sense to him then, and everything was harmonious, in balance. Now that he has agreed to marry them, the world has become disordered. Now the Friar rarely rhymes because he is out of balance.

8. His final couplet expresses why he is in such a hurry to marry them. Remember, they only met the night before. He fears that if he leaves them alone together they will have sex anyway, and so he tells them, **"For, by your leaves, you shall not stay alone / Till holy church incorporate two in one."** Because this ends the scene, the couplet acts as a conclusion - the Friar is certain their love is not love, but actually intense sexual desire.

Act 3 Scene 1

1. Shakespeare signals that Mercutio is out of control by making him lose control of language. He stops using iambic pentameter, and speaks in prose. This is also characteristic of characters with low status. So it suggests that Mercutio is giving up his status as a noble, and replacing it with the status of honour, pride and violence. These are the masculine traits which Tybalt favours. Perhaps Shakespeare is suggesting that this masculine world is not noble. He could be pointing out a major problem of patriarchal society, that it will always result in "quarrel" and conflict.

   Shakespeare emphasises this by making Benvolio keep iambic pentameter. This is because Benvolio is Mercutio's opposite, desperate to avoid violence, and urging Mercutio to come away to somewhere more private:

   > **"I pray thee, good Mercutio, let's retire.**
   > **The day is hot; the Capulets, abroad;**
   > **And if we meet we shall not 'scape a brawl".**

   This emphasises how the noble response to conflict is to avoid it. We might see this as a feminine perspective, in contrast to the male view of Tybalt and Mercutio. We also notice, however, that Benvolio is led by Mercutio, who refuses to "retire". Instead he tries to persuade Benvolio that he really wants to fight, and that violence is in his nature. It isn't. Benvolio is astonished to find himself described in this way: "am I such a fellow?" His actions show that he isn't.

2. Just in case we have missed it, Tybalt also speaks in prose when he speaks to Mercutio. The language of violence has taken on prose rather than iambic pentameter because Shakespeare signals that they are out of control. This is also characteristic of characters with low status. So it suggests that Mercutio is giving up his status as a noble, and replacing it with the status of honour, pride and violence. These are the masculine traits which Tybalt favours. Perhaps Shakespeare is suggesting that this masculine world is not noble. He could be pointing out a major problem of patriarchal society, that it will always result in "quarrel" and conflict.

3. **"Thou wilt quarrel with a man for cracking nuts, having no other reason but because thou hast hazel eyes."**

   Mercutio revels in conflict. We could say he turns every conversation into a conflict of some kind. Here he uses humour, as always, to portray Benvolio as seeking a "quarrel" at every opportunity. This is the opposite of the Benvolio we have seen in the play, permanently playing the role of peace keeper. Mercutio isn't wrong about Benvolio, he is trying to shape the world to his desires. We've seen how he wants Romeo to recognise his own sexual desire could be satisfied with Mercutio. Now, he wants a fight with the Capulets, and wants to persuade Benvolio, despite his request that they should "scape a brawl", that he actually wants to fight them.

4. Why is Mercutio so angry when Tybalt accuses him of consorting with Romeo? **"Consort? What, dost thou make us minstrels?"** A consort was a group of musicians playing the viol, a fiddle. But a consort was also the spouse of a king or queen. Both these descriptions suggest that Tybalt is attacking Mercutio's masculinity.

So Tybalt implies that Mercutio is like a wife to Romeo. The final meaning of "consort" is that Tybalt is accusing Mercutio and Romeo of playing together, so not just suggesting that he is sexually attracted to Romeo, but that it is reciprocated because they are lovers. There was no word for homosexuality in Elizabethan England. The idea that men would have erotic feelings for each other was not strange or uncommon. But it was seen as a private, youthful, sexual experimentation which would need to be put aside with manhood and marriage. What angers Mercutio, then, is that Tybalt is making his desire for Romeo public. This is even more distressing to him because Romeo never seems to acknowledge or return Mercutio's desires.

5. The homosexual overtones of Tybalt's and Mercutio's quarrel leads to the tragedy of Mercutio's death. Tybalt has never killed anyone before - his duels have been ritualised. This is why he has written to Romeo to make a formal challenge. It is why he can't simply draw his sword and fight Romeo now, he needs Romeo to verbally accept the challenge, otherwise the attack would be dishonourable and unmanly. Roemo's reply, using the "love" of gentlemanly courtesy sounds like an insult to Tybalt.

> **"Tybalt, the reason that I have to love thee**
> **Doth much excuse the appertaining rage**
> **To such a greeting."**

What can Tybalt make of this? Romeo means that he has to love Tybalt now as a member of his family, because of his marriage to Juliet. But of course, Tybalt simply thinks that Romeo is telling him that he loves him, expressing the erotic desire Tybalt had accused Mercutio of having. Perhaps it is this sexual slur which leads him to lose control and kill Mercutio when he is undefended.

6. Although Mercutio appears enraged enough to fight Tybalt, he has no intention of fighting a fatal duel. He makes this clear to Tybalt in advance, pointing out that he intends to draw only a little blood:

> **"Good King of Cats, nothing but one of your nine lives, that I mean to make bold withal, and, as you shall use me hereafter, dry-beat the rest of the eight."**

He would need to take the other "eight" lives to kill Tybalt, and intends only to "dry-beat" those lives. "Dry"-beat tells us that he doesn't want to inflict further wounds which would, in contrast, be wet with blood.

7. Tybalt breaks with his code of honour when he stabs Mercutio who was "hurt under your [Romeo's] arm". Mercutio blames Romeo, a signal that Romeo is the author of his own fate. Remember, had he not decided to attend to the ball, despite the warnings of his dream, Tybalt would never have challenged him. Mercutio also becomes part of Romeo's fate when he repeats **"a curse on both your houses".** This is exactly what happens in the tragedy of the lover's deaths. Mercutio's curse comes true.

8. Tybalt returns. Perhaps he feels that he has failed a test of honour, and the only way to restore his reputation is to fight again - this time fairly. We can also sense that both he and Romeo choose to fight because of their view of masculinity. Tybalt taunts Romeo **"Thou, wretched boy, that didst consort him [Mercutio] here"**, implying that Romeo was Mercutio's lover. Calling him "boy" also ridicules his manhood. Romeo, in turn, feels that his love for Juliet has made him "effeminate", making him less brave:

> **"Thy beauty hath made me effeminate**
> **And in my temper softened valour's steel!"**

So, he is not really seeking justice or revenge for Mercutio, but simply trying to restore his sense of self as a man: **"My reputation stained / With Tybalt's slander."** So perhaps Shakespeare is showing us that the real root cause of the tragedy is society's view of masculinity. Both men kill because they are trying to be respected as men.

9. Romeo does this, even though he knows he is challenging "black fate" again. He speaks of this in a rhyming couplet, as though knowing that he is choosing his own ending (because couplets usually mark the end of a scene):

> **"This day's black fate on more days doth depend.**
> **This but begins the woe others must end."**

The reference to "others" ending what he "begins" reveals that he knows his actions will end in death. He now believes in the portent of his dream, and is prepared to risk death. It is hubris to believe that he might survive this, and also not to think how this might affect Juliet.

10.   Romeo's cry, **"O, I am fortune's fool!"** is infuriating misdirection. The fricative alliteration blames fate. He doesn't want to accept any responsibility for the decisions he himself has made, and instead blames "fortune" for fooling him. Incredibly, he is wrong, and "fortune" actually saves his life. The Prince actually allows him to live, having promised to execute any further instigators of fights. And Romeo clearly challenged Tybalt. He should be executed. Instead, the Prince chooses mercy. His hubris is that he pretends "exile" is not mercy, **"Mercy but murders, pardoning those that kill."** His punishment, as he realises in Act Five, is that this won't just lead to Juliet's death, but also the death of another kinsman, Paris.

Act 3 Scene 2

1. Juliet's language, as she waits to have sex with Romeo, is filled with poetry. Although this reveals her excitement, Shakespeare makes sure it continually represents tragedy and death. She wants "night", when Romeo will come to her, to rush in. She imagines the Sun-God's son, Phaeton, speeding night towards them in his chariot. However, in Greek myth, Phaeton lost control of his father's chariot, spilling the sun, scorching the earth and killing the animals. This spillage also created the Milky Way. He is a symbol for lack of control, which suggests that Romeo is out of control. Similarly, perhaps Juliet is also dangerously out of control.

2. She describes Romeo in the same black and white imagery which he used to describe her when he first saw her:

"For thou wilt lie upon the wings of night
Whiter than new snow upon a raven's back."

The raven's blackness is a reminder of death, and we could argue that the surprising choice of "snow" in this hot summer also reminds Juliet of death. But though the colours are the same, the imagery is wildly different - Romeo imagined her as a "dove". She imagines him as "snow", which would presumably make her the "raven" in this image. These opposites remind us of the opposites who dominate the play, the Montagues and Capulets. It suggests that, despite their love, they aren't well matched. Remember the image the both had of themselves as the falconer and of their lover as the falcon?

3. She next imagines her own death, dying before Romeo. Then she imagines the gods making a constellation of stars in the shape of Romeo. This characterises Romeo as a hero of Greek myth, as so many of the myths explain the constellations, which are the origin of star signs. However, the Milky Way was formed in myth when Phaeton lost control of the sun's chariot. So the image of Romeo made into a constellation: **"Take him and cut him out in little stars"**, depends on a tragic mistake. Again, this indicates that their marriage is also a mistake. There is also an ironic sense that Juliet is bringing that fate closer, referring to the "stars" which will make them **"star-crossed lovers"**. She also imagines that her death will then cause the death of Romeo, which is exactly the fate that happens.

4. It is important to know that the marriage is not binding until the bride and groom have sex, and consummate it. This means that the tragedy is not inevitable yet. If Romeo is banished, Juliet can still marry Paris without losing her soul. Fate will still be satisfied - their love is still thwarted, "crossed", and Romeo's dream of death as a consequence of the ball is still true, because both Mercutio and Tybalt have died as a consequence of the ball.

5. Juliet describes her impatience and excitement in this simile, so she is as: **"an impatient child that hath new robes / And may not wear them."** By focusing on "child", Shakespeare points out the immaturity of their love, and their decision making.

6. The most startling aspect of this immaturity is the attraction of death. The Nurse enters wailing about Tybalt's death. The bitter comedy is that her poor word choice encourages Juliet to imagine it is Romeo who has died. But despite the violence between the families, Juliet's first thought isn't that Romeo has been killed. Instead she asks, **"Hath Romeo slain himself?"** It is as though she associates their love, and their hasty marriage, with an attraction to death. She associates their love with death. She thinks Romeo's impulsive character would choose suicide.

7. When Juliet finally learns that Romeo is alive, but has been banished for killing Tybalt, she echoes Romeo's poetry of Act One: **"Therefore do nimble-pinion'd doves draw Love, / And therefore hath the wind-swift Cupid wings"** and **"Beautiful tyrant! fiend angelical! / Dove-feather'd raven!"** Romeo crammed opposites together in his list of oxymorons, and Juliet does the same. His "feather of lead" is echoed by Juliet's "Dove-feathered raven". Marrying the opposites of "dove" and "raven" also shows the unnatural nature of their marriage as not suited to each other. Like Romeo's love, her rhymes reveal her immaturity.

So, why does Shakespeare give Juliet the same kind of poetry; what is unreal about her love? It makes us ask if what they are really in love with is death? Or if it is not love at all, but sexual desire.

8. Even in her grief, Juliet is still obsessed by Romeo's body. He has a "flowering face", is "beautiful", a **"moral paradise of such sweet flesh"** and a "gorgeous palace". The sibilance and alliteration all emphasise her desire for Romeo's body. If anything, killing Tybalt has made him more physically attractive to her.

9. She defends Romeo when the Nurse criticises him. Then she imagines that Romeo's banishment is a greater cause of grief than Tybalt's death: **"that one word "banishèd"/ Hath slain ten thousand Tybalts."** This hyperbole is shocking, and again points to her immaturity.

   But worse is to follow. Rather than have Romeo banished, she imagines a preferable alternative would be the grief she would feel if the Nurse had continued with '"Thy father" or "thy mother, nay, or both" are dead. On the one hand, this shows her passion for Romeo. But on the other hand, it suggests that a real motivation for her choice of husband, and for her haste to marry, is hatred of her parents. She would rather they were dead, and Romeo still in Verona.

10. Juliet appears to tell the Nurse that, now Romeo is banished, she will commit suicide: **"I'll to my wedding bed. / And death, not Romeo, take my maidenhead!"** But even now, her last words are about sex. She desperately wants to share her virginity, her "maidenhead" with Romeo. Shakespeare keeps contrasting the depth of her love with the extremes of her sexual desire. This prompts the Nurse to fetch Romeo, and keep Juliet alive, which suggests that she thinks Juliet's threat to kill herself is real.

Act 3 Scene 3

1. The Friar takes on the role of the Chorus, without knowing it. He tells Romeo that: **"Affliction is enamoured of thy parts, / And thou art wedded to calamity."**

   He means that Romeo is really married to his tragic fate. This suggests again that it isn't the killing of Tybalt that has made him "fortune's fool", it is going through with the marriage itself. Ironically, he is literally married to Juliet, as the Friar obviously knows, so he is also describing Juliet as "affliction" and "calamity". Patriarchal societies naturally describe female sin as much worse than male sin. Is Shakespeare attacking this view through the Friar (who we remember is wrong about so much to do with the lovers), or does he agree with it?

2. Well, Shakespeare pointedly goes on to give the Friar the voice of reason in this scene. We are encouraged to side with him. When Romeo decides that "banishment" is worse than "death" we might sympathise with the power of his emotions. But we also think this is sheer immaturity. The Friar agrees with us: **"Be patient, for the world is broad and wide."**

3. Romeo's endless bleating about banishment is ridiculous. He mentions the word "banishment" or "banish" eleven times in this scene, and this fixation is like dealing with a small child who can't let go of a perceived injustice.

4. The counterargument is the way Romeo describes the state of being young to engage our sympathy: **"Thou canst not speak of that thou dost not feel. Wert thou as young as I, Juliet thy love"**.

It is interesting that, as a young man, Romeo looks on adulthood as a time when feelings are less important. Alternatively, as a friar, Friar Lawrence will have taken a vow of chastity and so has lived a life without having a lover or a marriage. (This is a change from Brooke's poem, where he has a secret room in which he used to hide his lovers). Catholic hypocrites! Although this does make us more sympathetic to Romeo, he does display a terrible lack of logic. If adulthood stops people feeling as intensely as he does, perhaps he should not set so much store by his feelings and know that, in time, he will be able to deal with them better, because that what adults do. Or perhaps Shakespeare wants us to judge our youthful emotions as more pure.

5. I think we are supposed to despair at the behaviour of both lovers because their reactions are both extreme and childish. When the Friar describes Romeo to the Nurse, crying "on the ground", this acts as a stage direction. He is literally having a tantrum like a todler. The Nurse's description backs this up, with her repetition mimicking Romeo's repetitive crying:

> **"Blubbering and weeping, weeping and blubbering.**
> **Stand up, stand up. Stand, an you be a man.**
> **For Juliet's sake, for her sake, rise and stand.**
> **Why should you fall into so deep an O?"**

As usual with the Nurse, there must be comedy. Here it is the sexual puns she keeps making (possibly unconsciously). "Stand" has meant erection repeatedly since the opening scene. The 'O' was a reference to the vagina. Shakespeare had Mercutio introduce the "O" to us earlier, while he exaggerated the length of Romeo's penis in Act Two, Scene Three: **"O here's a wit of cheverel, that stretches from an inch narrow to an ell broad!"** (An "ell" was a unit of measure, 45 inches long).

Mercutio didn't make this up - it is a convoluted reference, perhaps referring to the shape of an O. Other slang for vagina was the 'O thing', because women had no-thing between their legs (in contrast to men). It's exhausting, isn't it? I feel Shakespeare wants us both to laugh and be exasperated at the constant fixation on sex.

Anyway, the Nurse, perhaps inadvertently, but perhaps deliberately, suggests that Romeo will feel much better once he and Juliet have had sex. Again, Shakespeare keeps undermining the lovers' feelings by asking if it is simply sexual desire. And he undermines their emotions through his use of humorous sexual innuendo. It leaves the audience constantly unbalanced, not sure how to react.

6. Shakespeare keeps us in this state through irony. Juliet had asked "what's in a name?" Now, she is in tears at the mention of his name. Romeo describes it with a violent metaphor:

> **"As if that name,**
> **Shot from the deadly level of a gun,**
> **Did murder her"**

Again, this is exactly what happens - by killing himself, Romeo does provoke Juliet's suicide, so in some sense the "name" Romeo does murder her.

7. Shakespeare also uses another of Romeo's metaphors to dismiss the lovers as immature: **"I have stained the childhood of our joy"**. Romeo means that their joy is still so young, as they have only just met. But the imagery also implies their joy is childlike, what we today would call puppy love.

8. The Friar also describes Romeo using The Great Chain of Being as a way to criticise his behaviour:

    > "**Art thou a man? Thy form cries out thou art.**
    > **Thy tears are womanish. Thy wild acts denote**
    > **The unreasonable fury of a beast.**"

    In this patriarchal society, men are superior to women, and women superior to animals. Reminding Romeo of this sets out his duty to behave as a man, by not committing suicide. It is interesting that, because society is patriarchal, the Friar imagines that simply reminding Romeo of his duty as a man will stop him committing suicide. The most important value in this society is being a man. Yet ideals of manhood have already led to the death of Tybalt and Mercutio, both of whom were pursuing honour and reputation: Tybalt by challenging Romeo's "sneer" at attending the ball, and Mercutio at Tybalt's sneer that Romeo and he "consort" as lovers. Shakespeare is certainly asking the audience if society has the right values attached to manhood.

9. A man would court a woman, exactly as Romeo was courting Rosaline, with gifts, compliments and perhaps poetry. When the Friar tells him **"Happiness courts thee in her best array"** his message is to be thankful that he is still alive. But by feminising "happiness" in this personification it again makes Romeo seem unmanly. Romeo will reject this in favour of the more masculine role of bridegroom, even though (or perhaps because) it will be the bridegroom of death, as he is "wedded to calamity". Partly this is proof of his immature attraction to death. But it is also partly because happiness does not appear to be valued in the patriarchal society, which is why it is given a female personification.

10.   The Friar is very keen for Romeo to return to Juliet. Partly this is to stop his talk of suicide. But more importantly for his plan, he needs Romeo to consummate the marriage. This will give it legal standing, which is why he talks about it being "decreed". This will allow him to use the marriage to put an end to the feud. Despite the fact that Romeo has killed Tybalt, he still thinks this is possible, which may be fanciful.

    > "**Go, get thee to thy love, as was decreed.**
    > **Ascend her chamber, hence, and comfort her.**"

Act 3 Scene 4

1. Like all the characters who meet a tragic fate, Paris also suffers from hubris. He appears to have used the death of Tybalt to pressure Capulet into bringing forward his marriage to Juliet. We have to infer this, because Shakespeare deliberately starts the scene in media res. He has to explain **"That we have had no time to move our daughter",** meaning to persuade her to marry.

    In Baz Luhrmann's film, Capulet is portrayed as drunk and a violent abuser of his wife and daughter, and this explains his sudden change of plan. But the text doesn't suggest this, other than Lady Capulet telling him he is "too hot". In the source poem, it is actually Lady Capulet's idea to marry Juliet to Paris. Shakespeare changes this to make the action more dramatic – over 5 days instead of 9 months. But it also allows him to attack the patriarchal arrangement of marriage and its damaging effect on daughters. When Tybalt died, Capulet lost a nephew and ally against the Montagues. Marriage to Paris will strengthen his social status, because Paris is related to the Prince. At the same time, the Montagues are weakened by the exile of Romeo.

But it isn't just fathers who are criticised. It is also the suitor. If Paris has not pushed for this marriage, then his fate does not seem justified. But because he dies as a result of the marriage, we can infer this must have been his idea, his hubris.

2. Capulet's hubris is that he no longer wants to ask Juliet to consider marriage to Paris. He tells Paris that he is certain she will go along with is decision:

> **"Sir Paris, I will make a desperate tender**
> **Of my child's love. I think she will be ruled**
> **In all respects by me. Nay, more, I doubt it not. —"**

The movement from "think" to "doubt it not" feels forced. Using the "desperate" to describe his offer of Juliet's love also unconsciously reveals his fear that he is making a mistake.

Act 3 Scene 5

1. Shakespeare places a "pomegranate tree" outside Juliet's window. This was used in Elizabethan art as a symbol of fertility, but also of eternal life, through belief in Jesus. This therefore implies God's blessing over the marriage, despite the fact that it will lead to tragedy. Fate is therefore also God's will, rather than simple punishment for hubris.

2. Romeo's language once again invites death: **"Come, death, and welcome! Juliet wills it so"**. This again is strangely prophetic, as when Juliet fakes her own death, she "wills it". We can even say that this also brings about Romeo's death.

3. Although Juliet tries to save Romeo's life by getting him to leave, her language also invites death: **"Then, window, let day in and let life out."** Romeo is let out of the window alive, but she also lets his life out - it is the last time she will see him alive.

4. This is not an accident. As Romeo climbs down to leave, Shakespeare gives her a simile which doesn't just hint at Romeo's death, but makes it seem inevitable:

> **"O God, I have an ill-divining soul.**
> **Methinks I see thee now, thou art so low**
> **As one dead in the bottom of a tomb."**

This is also highly specific - not just dead, but at "the bottom of a tomb". Again, this foreshadows exactly where he will die, and where he will lie next to her.

5. Juliet's conversation with her mother follows this same ironic template. The dramatic irony is that we know her words have a different meaning to those understood by Lady Capulet. But, a further level of irony is that we also know Juliet's fate, while she does not. So, when she says:

> "Ay, madam, from the reach of these my hands.
> Would none but I might venge my cousin's death!"

Her mother believes she wants Romeo dead. Whereas we know that she wants to get her "hands" on him because she is still thinking about the physical joys of sex. But, in drinking the Friar's potion, we also know "none but" she will cause Romeo to kill himself. This double layer of irony is a way to help us sympathise with the lovers, but also to distance us from them, because of our superior knowledge of their fate.

6. Juliet's deception is also sexual, which suggests again that sexual attraction is just as much of a motive for the marriage as love. She tells her mother:

> "To wreak the love I bore my cousin
> Upon his body that slaughtered him!"

The choice of verb, "wreak" suggests violence that is out of control, and is very surprising to use with "love". Again, Shakespeare gives her this word not just to show the extreme passion of their love, but the destructive nature of their desire - the lovers do not care what they destroy, even themselves.

7. Lady Capulet is also prophetic about how Romeo will die. She wants to hire an assassin to poison him, to **"give him such an unaccustomed dram".** Fate arranges for Romeo to do this himself. This prophecy is also applied to Juliet, when she refuses to marry Paris. This causes Lady Capulet to say: **"I would the fool were married to her grave!"** And of course, she is.

8. Capulet and Lady Capulet make no attempt to understand Juliet. Her mother tells her that the marriage to Paris must be **"a sudden day of joy"**, and the repetition of "joy" suggests she is trying to convince herself of this. Her father describes her with an extravagant metaphor, suggesting that her tears are as endless as the sea:

> "Evermore showering? In one little body
> Thou counterfeit'st a bark, a sea, a wind"

"Evermore" suggests his impatience with Juliet, even though Tybalt died only the day before; "counterfeit" suggests that she is being over emotional and faking the severity of her tears.

9. Capulet's disgust at Juliet's refusal of the marriage with Paris reflects the violence of patriarchal society towards women. Although he appears entirely unreasonable and "too hot" with rage, much of what he says is exactly how the patriarchal society deals with women.

> "But fettle your fine joints 'gainst Thursday next
> To go with Paris to Saint Peter's Church,
> Or I will drag thee on a hurdle thither."

To "fettle" here is to glaze the "joints" of pottery. This metaphor treats her as a simple possession which has been manufactured for sale - by her parents. But "fettle" had a more common meaning, to prepare for show. Here Capulet means the "fine joints" of her body. The fricative alliteration tells us exactly the purpose of these joints - he is thinking of her body as a sexual object which will both satisfy a husband and produce children.

Although it is highly unlikely that he would literally drag her to church, the "hurdle" was what traitors are tied to. Patriarchal society would view a noble daughter's refusal to marry as betraying the family's interests. Her only hope then would be to join a convent as a nun. Capulet's invective sounds very violent, but when he says **"my fingers itch"** he means he wants to hit her, but resists. After all, he needs to send her unblemished to her wedding.

He does give her an alternative to obeying him, which is to **"Graze where you will"**. Here "graze" marks her out as a farm animal, which emphasises her patriarchal duty to breed. Shakespeare is dramatising the exact predicament of a noble woman in Elizabethan England. Interestingly, the Elizabethan era saw changing social attitudes to marriage. It is entirely conceivable that Shakespeare and Anne arranged pregnancy to force their own families to allow their marriage. Women and men from low social status families would be much more likely to marry for love. But wealthy families concerned with increasing wealth, inheritance and influence would not. So, it is very possible that Shakespeare wants his audience to sympathise with the wealthy women who, in terms of marriage have less freedom than they do.

10.   Juliet turns to the Nurse, who advises her to marry Paris. She uses the metaphor an "eagle" to describe Paris, which fits perfectly with Juliet's metaphor of Romeo as a "falcon". The eagle is more regal and has higher status in The Great Chain of Being. This would be the patriarchal choice - Paris is a better match even if Romeo had not been a Montague, because a Count is superior to a Lord. However, to make a second marriage is the sin of bigamy, and Juliet's soul would go to hell. Juliet is astonished to hear the Nurse say this and asks: **"Is it more sin to wish me thus forsworn"**? Because hell is real in her world view, choosing to commit suicide is not a terrible alternative.

Act 4 Scene 1

1. Shakespeare focuses on fate approaching, so that we get a sense of the lovers being trapped. Throughout the play, Shakespeare teases us with 'if only' moments, where fate can still be avoided. Here, Juliet, Paris and the Friar exchange coded language:

> **PARIS: That "may be" must be, love, on Thursday next**
> **JULIET: What must be shall be.**
> **FRIAR LAWRENCE: That's a certain text.**

It is very unusual for Shakespeare to share the iambic pentameter between three characters. Even more unusual, they share a rhyming couplet. Usually couplets emphasise an ending of a scene. Here the ending hinted at is fate - "What must be shall be." Dramatic irony means that Paris reads this as Juliet's commitment to marry him on Thursday, whereas she means that she intends to kill herself. The Friar doesn't know this, but probably means that God, in the form of fate, has already decided how events will end. We, however, know this will result in the death of both lovers from the Prologue.

But notice that it is also the male characters who rhyme, not Juliet. This possibly reflects the male dominance of her society, and perhaps hints at a male cause of the tragedy.

2. Shakespeare definitely focuses on the power of men in this scene. Paris makes an extraordinary statement to Juliet: **"Do not deny to him that you love me."** First, he doesn't declare his love for Juliet.

   Next, he simply expects her love as a right. This feels like more than just assuming that love will follow marriage. It is as though he expects his high status, wealth and good looks will mean, in the patriarchal marriage market, that he is an irresistible catch. This reveals an incredible amount of vanity and arrogance: hubris. Shakespeare seems to be saying that this extreme arrogance is a natural consequence of the patriarchal control of women. After all, Paris's previous experience of women or teenage girls has probably been exactly what he expects from Juliet: he is such a desirable match that they do fall in love with him. Patriarchal society is set up to make this happen.

3. Juliet threatens to commit suicide if the Friar can't offer her a way out of the wedding to Paris. Her final demand is expressed as a couplet, emphasising that she means this really will be an ending - she will go through with killing herself:

   > **"Be not so long to speak. I long to die**
   > **If what thou speak'st speak not of remedy."**

   She also plants an idea with the word "remedy", hinting that the solution will be one of the remedies he makes as a herbalist. This immediately prompts him to think of the solution.

4. Again, Shakespeare plays with his characters. The Friar immediately decides to give Juliet a "liquor" which will make her appear dead for "two and forty hours". He introduces his plan:

   > **"I do spy a kind of hope,**
   > **Which craves as desperate an execution"**

   He imagines the "hope" is only a "kind of hope" because she will actually experience death for forty-two hours. But we know it is a kind of hope because there is no hope for her, she is going to die anyway. Shakespeare emphasises this as the Friar's language plays on the double meaning of "execution". He means to execute an action, to carry it out, but through dramatic irony, we understand that this is also bringing the execution of the lovers' lives closer.

   It is also worth considering that executions happen as a punishment. The lovers' fate is not being portrayed as unfair - Shakespeare is suggesting that they are also being punished for breaking, or transgressing against, social rules. In case we are unsure of this, notice how the Prince will end the play, saying "all are punished". "All" specifically includes Romeo and Juliet.

5. Friar Lawrence next comes up with a fully worked out plan. Not only does he have a vial of "liquor" which will do the job:

   - He also knows exactly how long the dose will work.
   - He has planned for the Nurse not to sleep with her, so she won't see Juliet drink from the vial.
   - He has thought through that the Capulets don't bury the dead, but display them in a "vault".

- He has thought through how he will let Romeo know, by "letters" and that Romeo himself will come to wake Juliet in her tomb, and take her to Mantua.

On the one hand this suggests that the Friar is highly intelligent and resourceful. But on the other hand, it suggests he is manipulative and possibly dangerous. Why does he have this "liquor"? How has he tested it? Presumably testing it on people would risk killing them. It presents the Friar as fiercely intellectual, and not really caring about people as much as he cares about the greater good. Presumably it is worth experimenting on people if the drug might have benefits. It is worth secretly marrying the two lovers if it might restore peace to Verona. This habit of playing with people's lives is, of course, hubris.

6. It is easy to see the Friar as being forced into this position by Juliet's threat of suicide. But look at what he says to her after he has outlined his plan:

> "If no inconstant toy, nor womanish fear,
> Abate thy valour in the acting it."

He is worried that she won't risk taking the drug which is like "shrunk death". It's clear that he thinks her talk of suicide is hyperbole, an insincere threat. Now he warns her not to act like a child. This is why he describes any fears as an "inconstant toy". Next, he belittles her courage as a woman, describing her "womanish fear". He manipulates her by appealing to the two things she resents most, being seen as a child, and merely female. Her parents, because society is patriarchal, treat her as a child, even though they are marrying her off. And society controls when and who she marries because that is the status of women.

7. A charitable view is that the Friar is manipulating her for her own good. If she marries Paris, her soul will go to hell. So this plot will save her soul. But the easiest way to keep her from hell would be to tell the Capulets and Montagues that he has already married Romeo to Juliet. This certainly wouldn't make life worse for the banished Romeo, and would save Juliet's soul. Who is he protecting then? Obviously, just himself. Shakespeare uses the Friar to criticise the Catholic church. On the surface, the Friar looks like he is interested in the common good. But beneath it, he is simply trying to save himself.

Act 4 Scene 2

8. When Juliet returns to her father, she tells him she is:

> "enjoined
> By holy Lawrence to fall prostrate here
> To beg your pardon. *(falls to her knees)*
> Pardon, I beseech you!"

This physical display of powerlessness and subservience is a shocking image of what the patriarchal nobility expects. Capulet just assumes that complete obedience to his wishes is natural, so he doesn't even reply to her at first. Instead he asks for the news of her submission to be sent to Paris. Capulet represents the male attitude in society, and Juliet represents the frightening loss of independence and agency suffered by women. Shakespeare wants the audience to see the injustice of male exploitation of women in society.

Act 4 Scene 3

9. Before Juliet drinks, she asks herself if the Friar would kill her with the drug in order to hide his part in the marriage. She decides that he is too "holy" for murder her. Then she imagines waking up in the tomb, next to the bones of her ancestors and the fresh corpse of Tybalt. Although in previous scenes her language has welcomed death - "I long to die" - now that she is facing death she feels fear and disgust. She imagines Tybalt's ghost "seeking out Romeo" for revenge. But more horrifying than this, she imagines waking with a kind of suicidal madness. She sees herself snapping off part of a skeleton and,

> **"with some great kinsman's bone,**
> **As with a club, dash out my desperate brains?"**

Shakespeare jolts us with this image. It suggests that Juliet's unconscious mind sees that her family will drive her to madness, and to suicide. This is also why she chooses a "kinsman'" rather than a kinswoman's bone, because it is the power of men in society which is causing her tragedy. We can also see her death as an attack on that male society - she is deliberately destroying a male skeleton. Shakespeare is criticising male power again.

Act 4 Scene 4

10.   This scene also begins with Shakespeare attacking male habits. It allows Shakespeare to offer a window into the marriage. When Lady Capulet suggests Capulet should get some sleep rather than stay up all night, he says he has been used to it. Lady Capulet observes **"Ay, you have been a mouse-hunt in your time"**. This metaphor characterises Capulet as a cat, and the "mouse-hunt" as pursuing women. It is casually dropped into conversation, as though this behaviour is totally normal for a husband. The implication is that he has only stopped because of his age and now even his wealth is not enough to make him attractive to young women.

A further implication is that wives simply have to put up with this. Capulet is actually delighted that his wife has brought it up. He sees it as proof that she loves him, and is jealous of the women he has sex with: **"A jealous hood, a jealous hood!"** We are reminded that both Romeo and Juliet focused on the word "faithful" when they made their vows love to each other. They aren't just rebelling against their parents because that's what teenage children do - they are rebelling against a corrupt and oppressive system they find immoral, because husbands are not required to be "faithful". How their parents' generation treats marriage and the rights of wives and daughters is what disgusts them most.

Act 4 Scene 5

1. Shakespeare loves to introduce comedy before tragedy. Here, the Nurse is just about to discover Juliet's death, so the comedy will provide an ironic contrast. The Nurse is excited that Juliet is going

to have sex again, this time with another man, Paris. She tells Juliet she will need her sleep because tonight will be her wedding night and,

> **"The County Paris hath set up his rest**
> **That you shall rest but little. —God forgive me"**

She realises this is sinful, which is why she asks for God's forgiveness. But Capulet sees the same behaviour in himself as entirely normal, and so does his wife. Men are supposed to have many sexual partners, whereas a wife is not. That's why he stages this moment directly after Capulet's happy admission of unfaithfulness.

2. The Capulets' grief at finding Juliet dead appears genuine. But whereas Lady Capulet finds herself unable to speak for a moment, Capulet is eloquent and speaks poetically in metaphor. And what is he thinking of? Sex. To tell Paris that Juliet is dead, he says:

> **"O son! The night before thy wedding day**
> **Hath death lain with thy wife. There she lies,**
> **Flower as she was, deflowered by him."**

It implies that the most important aspect of her death is how it affects male honour. Paris won't have the satisfaction of having sex with a virgin. He won't "deflower" her. But even worse than this, Death has already "lain with" Juliet, and "deflowered" her already. Death is personified as a male rival, who has proved more powerful than Paris. We can't help feeling disgusted by Capulet's focus. Shakespeare also adds irony to the image - Juliet has lost her virginity to Romeo, and when she lay with him, she lay with "death". It was her marriage to Romeo that has led to her taking the drug, and will lead to Romeo drinking his own poison, which will lead to Juliet's actual death.

3. Shakespeare ends the scene of the Capulets' grief with the Friar who typically cares little about people. He tells them:

> **"Heaven and yourself**
> **Had part in this fair maid. Now heaven hath all".**

Christianity offers this consolation. Remember that all Juliet's siblings have already died, and a high mortality rate for children was typical in Elizabethan England. Shakespeare was one of eight children. The first two died before he was born, as infants. Of the other five, one died aged seven. Knowing that these deaths were part of God's plan, and that their souls were safe in heaven does offer a kind of hope to the grieving family. But the Friar doesn't use any empathy or sensitivity here. He effectively tells them their grief is excessive and a cause of "shame". Shakespeare is perhaps pointing out how unfair the church is to treat grief in this way.

4. On the other hand, he also uses the Friar to criticise the patriarchal view of marriage. He implies that this arranged marriage to "advance" the parents' interests is corrupt. Consequently, he contrasts this with how God wants to "advance" Juliet:

> **"The most you sought was her promotion,**
> **For 'twas your heaven she should be advanced.**

And weep ye now, seeing she is advanced
Above the clouds, as high as heaven itself?"

We can sense his disgust at this patriarchal arrangement with the addition of "most". This emphasises how little Juliet's feelings matter. Comparing their desire for social "promotion" as their "heaven" also shows that their desires are sacrilegious, they go against God. This criticism is doubly powerful, as Catholics would be viewed by the audience as having false idols themselves, so for the Friar to criticise false worship means it must be doubly sacrilegious.

5. **"The heavens do lour upon you for some ill.**
   Move them no more by crossing their high will."

   The Friar exploits their grief to prepare them to reconcile with the Montagues. He tells them that God has chosen to take Juliet from them as a punishment for their sins. We can imagine he means the sin of arranging the marriage, when Juliet is so young, and also without her willing consent. So Shakespeare uses him to attack this patriarchal society. But there is an added criticism of the Friar, because he is of course manipulating them with lies.

6. The scene doesn't end here, as we might expect. In production, the rest of the scene with Peter and the musicians is often cut. But we have already seen that Shakespeare likes to introduce comedy before tragedy. So, before Romeo hears that Juliet is dead, we have the contrast of the banter of Peter forcing the musicians who arrived for the procession to the wedding to sing and play music for the funeral.

   Their last lines are: **"Come, we'll in here, tarry for the mourners and stay dinner."** This simply suggests that life goes on for the living. Perhaps there is another reason too. The servant class doesn't have the luxury of grief. They are worried about a lack of "silver" - if they don't play, they don't get paid, and then they can't afford food. This is why they think so much of their "dinner".

Act 5 Scene 1

7. As fate closes in on the lovers, so does the dramatic irony. Romeo in Mantua has dreamed that he is dead, and Juliet has come to him:

   "And breathed such life with kisses in my lips
   That I revived and was an emperor."

   The dream will come true - Juliet will find Romeo dead and kiss him. But this will not "revive" him. In Act 1, Romeo's dream warned him, and gave him an opportunity to change his fate. Now, his dreams taunt him, offering him a false hope. This emphasises how Romeo is being punished for his hubris. As soon as he hears of Juliet's death, Romeo understands this straight away. He attacks fate, **"Then I defy you, stars!"** This defiance only works if he believes fate has planned some other way for him to die - his defiance is to die on his own terms, at Juliet's side.

8. Romeo decides to buy poison from an apothecary. Shakespeare could make the apothecary a rich man, used to selling poisons to rich Italian nobles so that they could assassinate their rivals. During the previous century, the two most famous families in Italy had been the Borgias and Medicis,

both famous for poisoning their rivals and enemies. We also know that Lady Capulet has her own apothecary from whom she can buy poison to kill Romeo. So, a rich apothecary would suit Shakespeare's criticism of the Italians and their Catholic hypocrisy. But instead he decides that the apothecary is only giving Romeo poison because he is poor:

> **"Contempt and beggary hangs upon thy back.**
> **The world is not thy friend nor the world's law."**

So it seems a main reason to introduce his poverty is to give us some social commentary. This contrasts to the nobles in the play who are obsessed with honour and status, while the poor are reduced to poverty and "famine".

The apothecary is highly skilled, but is still like a "beggar". Another reason might be to contrast him with the Friar. Friar Lawrence, as a herbalist, is very similar to the apothecary. Perhaps Shakespeare is also using this to attack the Catholic monasteries. Not only were they hugely wealthy, but their monks and friars took the livelihoods of any rivals. The apothecary has to earn a living and pay for premises, where all this is provided for the Friar.

The monastery could therefore undercut the working man - they farmed and produced significant crops, cheeses, beers and wines, and of course herbalists. Their industry was subsidised by the church's wealth, while the poor had higher costs and therefore couldn't compete. When Henry VIII destroyed the monasteries, he wanted that wealth for himself, and he needed the freedom to act without having to defer to a Pope in Rome. But perhaps an unintended consequence of this was the huge opportunities the dissolution of the monasteries offered to ordinary people trying to set themselves up in business without unfair competition. Shakespeare could be celebrating this.

Act 5 Scene 2

9. We meet Friar John, who Friar Lawrence had entrusted to deliver his letter to Romeo, explaining the plan to "wake" Juliet from her drugged "death". But fate has intervened. He was prevented from leaving by a suspected case of the plague:

> **"Where the infectious pestilence did reign,**
> **Sealed up the doors and would not let us forth."**

But this also offers an alternative view of the monasteries. Friar John had been trapped in this house because he went to find a "barefoot" Friar, who was "visiting the sick" with "pestilence" which could have been plague. This friar is heroic - he has taken a vow of poverty, which is why he doesn't wear shoes. His mission is to help the sick, despite the very real risks to his own life. And this risk is doubled because once a case of plague is suspected, everyone is locked in the house until a quarantine period has passed.

This was a cheap health service which England lost once the monasteries were destroyed. Although Shakespeare knows his audience will mainly be made up of anti-Catholic protestants, there will be many who still mourn the loss of the way of life they offered.

Some historians also speculate whether Shakespeare was himself a Catholic. When he lived in London, he sent all his profits back to Stratford to invest in properties and farmland. He lived in cheap lodgings, like a modern-day student, right up until he retired from writing plays. But then he did invest in London property, buying up the Gatehouse to a Dominican priory known as "Blackfriars". Since 1590 it had been a place where Catholics met in secret to worship (as they were prohibited from practising their faith). In 1623 the top floor collapsed during a service and 90 Catholic worshippers were crushed to death.

Challenging his audience's assumptions is a constant feature in this play. Act Five is the most political, as we have seen with the portrayal of the apothecary as a poor victim in society. Shakespeare seems to be asking his audience whether they are really better off without the monasteries - no one has replaced the Friar's helping plague victims in their own homes.

10.   The Friar asks Friar John to bring him a "crow", meaning a crowbar to break into the Capulet vault. Romeo gives two different names for these instruments, a "mattock" and "wrenching iron", because Shakespeare wants us to know that calling it a "crow" is significant." It is symbolic, reminding us of the language used to describe Juliet's rivals and it is, of course, a motif of death. So, symbolically, it means that Friar Lawrence will carry death with him to Juliet. She will die partly because of him.

Act 5 Scene 3

1. Many productions want to reunite Romeo with Juliet for the final tragedy of true love quickly. Introducing Paris, who also appears to be in love with Juliet, is problematic, so his part in the scene is often cut. This is a pity. Let's think about some patriarchal reason why he is outside her tomb.

   He speaks to her from outside, "Sweet flower, with flowers thy bridal bed I strew—". The repetition of flowers isn't necessary - the audience can see them clearly. Instead, it is to remind us of Capulet's description of the dead Juliet as a flower, "deflowered" by death. Even in death, he still wants to control her body. The flowers are a symbol of Juliet's virginity, which he can never possess.

2. Shakespeare contrasts Juliet's relationship to her father with Romeo's relationship with his. Romeo tells Balthasar,

   > **"Hold, take this letter. Early in the morning**
   > **See thou deliver it to my lord and father."**

   Although he is committing suicide, he still thinks of his parents. His measure of respect, calling his father "my lord" makes clear that his suicide is not an act of rebellion against his parents. Whereas, with Juliet, we can certainly argue that she is motivated in part by rejecting her parents because she resents being the victim of their patriarchal control. But Shakespeare also attacks the patriarchy through Romeo. Romeo deliberately writes to his father, rather than his mother, because his father has higher status in Romeo's mind. To highlight the injustice of this, Shakespeare will introduce a twist. Romeo's mother has already died, apparently from grief that he has been exiled. So we can argue he has deliberately ignored the parent who loved him most, because his mother is female.

3. Romeo has to hide his intention to commit suicide from Balthasar. He needs a plausible excuse. So he gives him a patriarchal reason for wanting to break into the tomb and be left alone. It is all about property:

> **"But chiefly to take thence from her dead finger**
> **A precious ring, a ring that I must use"**

In other words, he has to speak in a language that Balthasar will understand. He says he still wants to own part of Juliet, which to Balthasar makes sense, because that's the way males in this sort of society might behave. They own women through marriage. No one has tried to break in to own any part of Tybalt, or to guard his body in the same tomb, because he is a man.

4. Unlike Capulet, the patriarchal villain, Romeo does not personify death as a rival lover who has stolen his bride. Shakespeare shows that he is not as infected by a patriarchal perspective as Capulet and Paris. He imagines death as a creature whose hunger has been satisfied with Juliet's death. Romeo is going to force feed it his own body, **"I'll cram thee with more food!"**

5. From the perspective of tragedy, Paris must die as punishment for his hubris in pushing forward the marriage, and for his arrogance in taking Juliet's love for granted. Fate has also enlisted the help of masculine honour and the Prince, Paris's relative. When he intercepts Romeo he naturally thinks that Romeo is going to attack the bodies of Tybalt and Juliet. Paris also considers it his duty to arrest Romeo:

> **"Condemnèd villain, I do apprehend thee.**
> **Obey and go with me, for thou must die."**

Romeo has no desire to fight him, but fate urges Paris on until Romeo is forced to kill him. Shakespeare is perhaps critical of Paris for doing this – his first line has 11 syllables, and there are three consecutive stresses in "Condemnèd villain". Romeo is desperate to avoid this "sin" and even confesses that he plans to break into the "vault" in order to commit suicide: **"For I come hither armed against myself."** But Paris ignores this because he wants to "apprehend" Romeo in line with the Prince's orders. So, another ironic twist is that the Prince is partly responsible for Paris's death.

6. Astonishingly, Paris's dying words are a request for Romeo to bury him with Juliet. Even more astonishingly, Romeo agrees, and carries his body into the Capulet tomb. This really does get in the way of the love story we are expecting, and you can see why this scene is normally cut from modern performances.

So, what might Shakespeare have been thinking? Well, it's because this is a tragedy. Romeo makes the promise to bury him here because he realises Paris is a fellow victim of fate: **"One writ with me in sour misfortune's book"**. Romeo understands that his life is not just a love story, but a tragedy in which hubris is punished. Because he, Juliet and Paris are all linked in tragedy, Romeo is happy for their bodies to lie together.

7. Romeo personifies death as an invading army which Juliet has fought and lost to:

> **"Thou art not conquered. Beauty's ensign yet**
> **Is crimson in thy lips and in thy cheeks,**
> **And death's pale flag is not advancèd there. —"**

The "ensign" is the "flag" containing the army's insignia, commonly called colours. So he imagines that Juliet is not fully defeated. Though her breath is gone, her beauty still defies death. This military image is stereotypically male. Perhaps Shakespeare is again pointing out that the patriarchal nature of society is the most powerful cause of Juliet's fate. Even in love, Romeo can't let go of violent, masculine imagery.

He kisses Juliet. This symbolises both his love for Juliet, and his love of death. This is why he sees the kiss as a bargain with death:

> **"seal with a righteous kiss**
> **A dateless bargain to engrossing death."**

Perhaps Shakespeare portrays love as like the death of the self. The lover becomes so obsessed with the person whom they love that they lose their identity. The self dies. Or perhaps he is suggesting that the passions of love are extreme, and therefore destructive. This portrays the passions of young love as uncontrolled, and therefore always a mistake.

8. Shakespeare refuses to make this just a story about love. We might expect Juliet to wake now and find Romeo still dying beside her. She would talk to him as he died. To do this would emphasise her love and grief, and portray suicide as an uncalculated emotional response to his death.

   But instead, he introduces the Friar. This is another turning point of the play, as the Friar can save her life. But Shakespeare presents him as a manipulative coward. Instead of reuniting her with her family, he decides to hide her away:

   > **"Come, I'll dispose of thee**
   > **Among a sisterhood of holy nuns."**

   His choice of "dispose" rather than conceal reveals how little he cares about her feelings or her future. It also shows that he is simply protecting himself from the consequences of his part in the tragedy being known. Unsurprisingly, Juliet doesn't see a lifetime of celibate seclusion as an attractive alternative to an eternity with Romeo in death. Now there are two other reasons to kill herself. The life of nun is deeply unattractive. But the other is that both she and Romeo are also in love with death.

9. Juliet kills herself symbolically with Romeo's dagger:

   > **"O happy dagger,**
   > **This is thy sheath. There rust and let me die."**

   With this reference, Shakespeare points out that he could have left some poison behind to kill Juliet. After all, the apothecary told Romeo that he had enough to kill "twenty" men, so Juliet could easily have died from drinking a drop or two of unused poison. But instead, Shakespeare wants her to have to use Romeo's dagger. This unites them in death - she literally dies with part of him in her heart.

The "dagger" and "sheath" of her body are a metaphor for sexual union. The word "die" also had a sexual interpretation at the time, meaning to climax. To Juliet, her death is like a sexual union with Romeo. But the dagger and sheath are also a metaphor for how Romeo has killed Juliet. This imagery blames Romeo as the original cause of the tragedy. She calls the dagger "happy" because it is delivering to her the death that she wants. But this love of death starts with Romeo. Death was the warning he received in his dream, and rather than turning away from Capulet's ball, he chose death.

10. **"heaven finds means to kill your joys with love!**
And I, for winking at your discords, too
Have lost a brace of kinsmen. All are punished."

The ending offers the catharsis of tragedy. The Prince points out that everyone guilty of hubris has been punished by fate. Fate here is God's will, which is why they are killed by "heaven".

The Prince realises his tolerance of the feud, which he describes as "winking at discords", means that his hubris has been punished by Mercutio's and Paris's deaths. But more than that, "All are punished".

Because a tragedy tries to alleviate feelings of despair at the end, Capulet and Montague agree to build a "golden statue" of each other's child as they put aside their "enmity".

We expect some irony here, and we get it. The lovers' deaths have created the very world that would have allowed them to marry and be in love.

But wait Shakespeare, do you mean that the Friar gets off scot-free? He refuses to tell us. He teases us again. The Prince ends with an ambiguous statement: "Some shall be pardoned, and some punishèd."

In order for us to reach a state of catharsis, and purge ourselves of negative emotions, we have to decide what happens to the Friar for ourselves. We have to decide who is "pardoned" because they are innocent victims of fate, and those who are "punished" because of their hubris.

Part 2: Context

Top Ten Context 1597

1. Literacy

What would have happened if the servant could read? He wouldn't have had to show his list of invitations to Romeo, and Romeo would never gone to the ball. No tragedy! It all starts because of illiteracy. We can imagine how important this was to Shakespeare, because literacy is how he earned his living. It is an interesting question whether his daughters learned to read – there is no historical record to tell us.

2. The earthquake of 1580 was obviously terrifying. Although the play is not about fear, that is what people were feeling about the future. The Armada had invaded in 1588, and the country had been partly saved by bad weather. The Catholics countries of Europe were very likely to invade.

3. Civil War

The worry of Elizabeth's death without an heir threatened peace at home. Would there be civil war to find a successor? This fear is mimicked in the feud – two halves of the same city pitted against each other.

4. Duelling had come to England in the last 50 or 60 years from Italy. It was part and parcel of the idea of the courtly gentleman – the idea being that, as a gentleman's reputation needed to be courteous, honourable and gentle, they would go out of their way to behave in courteous, honourable and gentle ways. This minimised the danger of arming every gentleman with daggers and swords. The duel was seen as the ultimate deterrent. If you insulted someone, you knew this might lead to your death, which is why you would choose to compliment them instead. This is why Mercutio calls Tybalt the **"captain of compliments"**.

5. The Feud Between the Long and Danvers Families

The famous feud in Shakespeare's time involved two noble families, the Longs and the Danvers. Both families had influence at court. Like the Montagues and Capulets, it began with general brawling involving the servants. It led to legal battles in London and was already well known before it turned to tragedy.

The tragedy began as a duel of honour in 1594. Henry Long was dining in an Inn with his brother Walter. Charles and Henry Danvers entered with about seventeen followers. Charles struck John, which was of course a challenge. Henry Long drew his sword and wounded Charles in seven places. At this point Henry Danvers saved his brother's life by shooting Charles in the chest and killing him. The brothers then fled to France.

These events were incredibly topical and still scandalous in 1595, so Shakespeare has made the duelling incredibly topical. There is no duel in the original Brooke poem. But these events also echo Tybalt's murder of Mercutio, where he ignored the honourable rules of the duel. This is mirrored in the actions of Henry Danvers simply shooting Henry Long. Shakespeare is probably pointing out the impossibility of violence being controlled in a ritual way. The duel doesn't settle matters of honour – it leads to further dishonour. This image of the courtly gentlemen resorting to the ritual of a duel is shattered by how easily it turns to simple murder.

6. The Dissolution of the Monasteries

By 1534 King Henry had had enough of being a Catholic King. Problem number one, the church was Catholic, and the church was controlled by a foreign Pope. Problem number two, the church earned an absolute fortune, and Henry couldn't tax it. Problem number three, he had no male heir. Having been married to Catherine of Aragon since 1503, with only a daughter Mary as a reward, he needed a new wife. The Pope told him that as a Catholic, he could not remarry. So, that was that. In 1534, the Act of Supremacy made him head of the Church of England. Two Acts of Supremacy in 1536 and 1539 enabled him to start selling off the church's assets – there were 900 monasteries, friaries, priories, convents and abbeys.

While many people thought that the Catholic church was corrupt, taking too much money from the people, there wasn't widespread support for destroying it in the way Henry did. However, Henry simply executed those who opposed him.

In those 900 institutions, 10,000 religious men were in holy orders. Suddenly they were all unemployed. This was a big deal when the adult male population was only 500,000. It meant 1 in 50 were suddenly jobless and homeless.

The monasteries had also provided hospitals, and had fed and looked after beggars – in other words, looked after the poor. Suddenly, that was all gone.

Over time, hospitals were taken on by rich patrons, and the monastic grammar schools and charitable giving for beggars were paid for by the rich, but not as extensively as the church had done.

So, quite apart from the religious shock of having to reject being a Catholic, there was also a strong social shock in services and ways of life which had been changed. You can imagine that even 50-60 years later, in 1595, many families would miss what men like Friar Lawrence provided.

On the other hand, the Catholic religion had been successfully painted as the enemy. It helped, of course, that the enemy had launched a massive attack which might have overcome our navy. The 1588 Armada invasion could so easily have succeeded. What cause it to fail? Well, English Protestant brilliance of course. And the weather – a storm from God.

7. The Spanish Armada Attack 1588

130 Spanish galleons sailed into the channel. Although loaded with soldiers, they didn't invade. Who knows what would have happened if they had invaded straight away. The smaller English ships were more manoeuvrable and able to inflict more damage than the Spanish could return, but they couldn't stop the fleet or prevent a landing invasion. Fortunately, the Armada had order to wait instead at Calais, to prepare to take on board an army from the Netherlands. The English sent in fireships at night, and the Spanish fleet scattered in panic, cutting their anchors. A naval battle followed in which the Spanish lost 5 ships.

But then heavy winds sent the Spanish fleet north, around Scotland and Ireland. The winds became a storm, and many of the damaged ships sank as they couldn't drop anchor in shelter. Of the 130 ships which set off, only 67 returned to Spain.

In the next year, 1589, the English launched their own 'counter armada' with 150 ships. This was largely a failure, and 40 English ships were sunk or captured. Not only was England still open to invasion, but the royal finances were running low having spent a fortune on the naval campaigns.

In 1595 the English were constantly living with this threat, knowing that further attacks would come. And they did in 1596 and 1597.

8. Infant Mortality

14% of children died before their first birthday. A further 16% died before their fifteenth birthday.

A mother had on average 7 to 8 live births, over the course of 15 years of childbearing. Around 1 in 40 mothers died in childbirth.

We can infer from this that the Capulets have been particularly unlucky in the number of their children who have died. It also hints that Lady Capulet has probably stopped getting pregnant because her husband is now too old.

9. Plague

There were regular outbreaks of plague in London, where all public gatherings would be prohibited. This meant that all the playhouses were shut. The latest plague had been in 1592 and 1593, where 15,000 people died in London, and 4900 in the surrounding area. These numbers might not feel huge, but they are. There were only 150,000 people in the city of London, so one in ten people were killed. Many of the wealthy left London until the plague disappeared, but the poor could not afford to, and were therefore more likely to die.

Introducing the plague isn't just a plausible plot device which stops Romeo getting his letter from the Friar. Shakespeare uses it to heighten the feeling of impending disaster in the play by tapping in to the so recent memories of disaster his audience has just experienced.

10. The Wet Nurse

Breastfeeding is about 99% effective at preventing a woman getting pregnant. Because the patriarchal society needed a male heir to inherit wealth and family titles, the pressure was on to have a boy. Because infant mortality was high, the pressure was on to have more than one boy. So, if you married into a wealthy family, your husband would be pretty keen to get you reproducing again pretty quickly. Breastfeeding was a barrier.

No problem, your husband has plenty of money. Like Lord Capulet, you could pay for a woman who is already lactating to breastfeed your child. She is the Wet Nurse. If you want to stop her also feeding other people's babies and devoting herself to yours alone, well you could afford to have her live in your household too.

We can imagine that Juliet (as the oldest child), would then have passed the Nurse on to her brothers or sisters, until they died and Lady Capulet stopped getting pregnant. By the time the play opens, the

Nurse has a totally different role – she is a companion and chaperone to Juliet. Once Juliet is married, she will have no role in the Capulet household. Her main hope of being a paid servant is probably to follow Juliet when she marries. So, sticking close to her and falling in with her risky plans to marry are probably a risk which the Nurse feels she has to take to secure her own future.

Top Ten Features of the Patriarchy

1. Parents choose who their children will marry. The selection is made based on the quality of the alliance which can be made with the spouse's family. This quality is measured by social status and wealth.

2. The father of the bride will pay a substantial dowry to the groom, as a way to sweeten the deal. This can be in the form of money and property. When Shakespeare's father, John, got into financial difficulties, he took out loans secured against his wife Mary's dowry.

3. Men expect their brides to be virgins when they marry. Partly this is about control - the man wants proof that he is the most important male in his wife's world. It is also about ownership - the woman gives her virginity, and the man takes it. Once she has lost it, it is as though he owns it forever. Another practical reason is that the first-born son will inherit the father's property. So, the new husband will want to feel certain that he is the father of his child.

4. In order to preserve a daughter's virginity, they live constrained lives. They are always in the presence of other women - chaperoned - so that there is no occasion when they are alone with a man. This also applies to leaving the house, visiting the market, or friends.

5. Girls are expected to work on skills which will make them more desirable, both sexually and practically. They can learn arts and crafts - they might draw, damce, sing, embroider, and sew. But they are rarely if ever taught to read and write. They are therefore educated at home, perhaps with tutors, while boys can be both tutored and attend schools.

6. A woman's chastity becomes a valuable commodity. Their attractiveness is accompanied by their modesty, a lack of flirtation, a devotion to the husband and the family. As Capulet shows us, a man is valued for his stereotypically male attributes - his skill in his work, in fencing, his virility and his pursuit of other women or prostitutes.

7. Before Shakespeare's time, prostitution was controlled by the Church. Prostitution was allowed in brothels outside of the city walls in Southwark, and the brothels were inspected weekly to ensure that men stayed overnight, and therefore a prostitute had only one client per day. This limited the transmission of sexual diseases. The Church also made sure no women were forced into prostitution.

But by Shakespeare's time, many brothels had been closed and many more women became freelance prostitutes. Syphilis was the most serious sexually transmitted disease, which often ended years later in blindness, drooling and shaking. The disease first broke out in 1495 in Italy and spread across Europe. Consequently, men were faced both with easy access to prostitution, and frightening consequences of venereal disease. Rich men would therefore keep a courtesan - a high class prostitute who remained faithful to the man who paid for her lifestyle. Both these examples are ways in which men in a patriarchal society were able to treat women as property, to be bought.

8. One of the ways we can measure social change for women is the average age of marriage. Over the course of the 1500's, the average age went from 21 to 25, whereas in Italy the average age was closer to 20. Shakespeare appears to be ridiculing the Italian tradition of marrying young. This is why we find out Juliet is two weeks shy of being fourteen. He also lets us know that Juliet's mother was already pregnant with Juliet at the same age, and that Capulet believes this may have been a mistake. He tells Paris, "And too soon marred are those so early made" into wives. Partly this ridicules Italians. More importantly it deliberately asks the audience to think how far women should have independent lives of their own, and how far their identity should depend on the fathers who control them, and the men they marry.

9. Original Sin. You just can't trust a woman. It was no accident that Satan, in the form of a serpent, approached Eve rather than the noble, honourable Adam. Yes, he persuaded Eve to eat the forbidden fruit and then *she* persuaded Adam. Mankind's fall from God's grace is therefore Eve's fault. And because all women are descended from Eve, they are obviously more attracted to evil than men are. God certainly took this view, so he gave women the extra punishment of menstruation and childbirth. (The poor old serpent, who was simply an innocent bystander also suffered a terrible punishment. Until Satan impersonated him to seduce Eve, the serpent had four legs. God took them all away!) Women's greater sin is why. This is why marrying in secret is Juliet's idea. This is why Romeo wants to kiss her hand and see where that takes him, but Juliet holds out till she can kiss his lips. This is why the Nurse helps her, and keeps talking about sex, and gets the ladder which allows Romeo to climb to Juliet's balcony and consummate the marriage. This corresponds to the social perception that women are untrustworthy, especially in matters of sex and deception.

10. Mothers in rich families need to produce an heir. And at least a spare because, you know, infant mortality! So they become baby factories. The Wet Nurse is hired to take over breastfeeding the baby. This gives the wife both more energy and time for sex. But more importantly, that sex is not just recreational. Because the wife stops breastfeeding, her hormones return to normal and she is able to get pregnant again.

Top Ten Changes to Brooke's 3,020 line poem, *The Tragicall Historye of Romeus and Juliet* (1562)

1. The main source of the play was a poem written in 1562 by Arthur Brooke. His poem is deeply critical of the lovers and what he sees as their dishonesty and lust. It also attacks the Catholic church:

He is appalled by "the lusts of wanton flesh", and the lovers who **"have yielded their liberty thrall to foul desires".** So, he wrote his poem to **"teach men to withhold of themselves from the head long fall of loose dishonesty… And to this end (good reader) is this tragical matter written, to describe unto thee a couple of unfortunate lovers thralling themselves to unhonest desire, neglecting the authority and advice of parents and friends, conferring their principal councils with drunken gossips, and superstitious friars…"** Shakespeare makes sure that we have to think through our own moral stance - so the lovers aren't simply criticised for deceiving their parents. The prologue presents the parents as partly responsible, and the Capulets' patriarchal control of Juliet also makes us more sympathetic to her.

2. The monasteries and friaries had been taken over by the crown by 1541. Friars seem to have been less popular than monks, because they earned money from legacies – they encouraging the old to leave them wealth in their wills, instead of passing it on to their relatives. Shakespeare is critical of the Friar, but also gives him many words of wisdom. Brooke's Friar is also a hypocrite. He hides Romeo in a secret room where he used to hide women he was having sex with, quite against his religious orders. Shakespeare doesn't make Lawrence a hypocrite, but an arrogant schemer who tries to do good through his plotting.

3. Brooke does not mention that Rosaline is a Capulet, so Shakespeare added this to make us question what motivates Romeo.

4. The action in the poem takes several months – Romeo and Juliet are married for 3 months. Shakespeare compresses time to be closer to the unities of tragedy.

5. In Brooke's poem, Tybalt does not recognise Romeo at the ball. Paris isn't with the Friar when Juliet arrives. These details reveal how Shakespeare chose to speed up the action, by adding layer upon layer of conflict.

6. In the poem, Romeo kills Tybalt when he tries to defend himself in a larger fight, like the one in Act 1 Scene 1. There is no mention of Mercutio, and therefore no revenge for Tybalt killing him. Shakespeare changes this to emphasise the hubris of each of these male characters. They all meet the same fate because of their hubris. He also wants to challenge the male values of honour and violence.

7. Brooke constantly refers to fate, to "fortune" and the feud as being responsible for the deaths. Shakespeare shows all the characters' choices as just, if not more important, than fate or the feud.

8. In Brooke's poem the Friar goes unpunished, but the apothecary is hanged. The nurse is banished. Shakespeare instead invites the audience to decide on their own moral standpoint by refusing to tell us what happens to them. Romeo's speech about the apothecary's poverty also seems to make a social point, that he is forced into poverty by the monopoly of the church on medicine.

9. In the poem, Mercutio also tries to seduce Juliet – she actually sits between him and Romeo, and each grabs one of her hands. In the play Mercutio instead sees women as rivals who have taken Romeo away from him, introducing the theme of male love. Shakespeare introduces Juliet and Rosaline as rivals to Mercutio's love of Romeo, which increases the complexity of character and conflict.

10. In the poem, Juliet speaks first to Romeo – she takes the lead. Although Romeo speaks first in the play, the poem means that the audience will pick up on the skill Juliet uses to guide Romeo towards kissing her, rather than just her hand. Shakespeare also changed Juliet's age from 16. Partly this is to make Juliet more innocent. But it is also to make the idea of her marrying Paris more troubling, and Shakespeare uses this to criticise the patriarchal control of daughters. In the poem, it is Juliet's mother who comes up with the idea to stop Juliet's grief by arranging for her to marry Paris. She does this some time after the death of Tybalt. Shakespeare makes his change, introducing Paris before Juliet meets Romeo. Then he makes sure it is her father's idea. This is because he wants to show how damaging male power is in a patriarchal society, and Capulet represents the cruelty of how that power is used.

Top Ten Context of Shakespeare's Life

1. Shakespeare married Anne Hathaway when she was already three months pregnant. He was 18 and she was 26. We can certainly see this as a love match. Or, we can see it as a mistake.

2. Shakespeare never bought a home in London, despite being the equivalent of a millionaire. Instead, he sent all his money home to Stratford, and in 1597, bought the second largest house in the town, New Place, for his wife and children. So perhaps we can see this as a mark of his true love.

3. Shakespeare bought the Gatehouse to Blackfriars Friary once he moved back to Stratford. This large building was well known as a refuge and secret place of worship for Catholics, leading many critics to wonder if Shakespeare himself was secretly a Catholic. This might explain why his version of the Friar is much more sympathetic than in Brooke's source poem.

4. William had four sisters, but only one, Joan, survived. This might help us see Juliet as similar to his own sister.

5. Over two thirds of Shakespeare's love sonnets were written to a "fair boy". Many scholars speculate about who this might be, and whether they reveal Shakespeare's real feelings of love towards another man. These don't prove that Shakespeare was bisexual, but they certainly point us that way. This fits the theme of homosexual desire introduced with Mercutio, which certainly isn't in Brooke's poem.

6. Shakespeare had only three children, Susan, and two twins, Hamnet and Judith. This means that Anne possibly got pregnant only twice (though she may have had miscarriages). In any event, it is quite possible that Shakespeare was much less interest in heterosexual relations with his wife.

7. Was Shakespeare bisexual? Most modern scholars think he probably was. We can't take the plays as proof, because there are so many characters of all types, that it would be impossible to pick and choose which ones reflect him. For example, there are 9 references to hedgehogs in Shakespeare's plays, and they are all negative. Can we then say Shakespeare must therefore hate hedgehogs!

But if we look at the over 180 sonnets he wrote, we see Shakespeare mainly or entirely writing as himself. From these, most modern critics see Shakespeare as loving both men and women at the same time. These are often categorised as 'Fair Youth' sonnets, written to a beautiful young man, and 'Dark Lady' sonnets, written to a woman with black hair and brown skin.

8. There are over 50 references to falconry in Shakespeare's plays, which makes it possible that this was a pastime of his. This was mainly a sport of the rich, mainly because of the cost of training and maintaining the birds. The references which Romeo and Juliet use mark them out as rich and noble. But they also link to the idea of the hunt. When they see themselves as the hunter, and their lover as the hawk, what does the metaphor mean? At the very least it suggests that they are both trying to control and manipulate the other. In this way Shakespeare asks us to look beyond their love and ask what other motives they have. Romeo is certainly motivated by wealth and sex. Juliet is motivated by sex and independence from her family and the prospect of marrying Paris.

9. Shakespeare had only three children, and two of these were twins. This is an exceptionally low number for the time. One possibility is that this indicates a lack of sexual interest in Anne once he moved to London as a playwright.

10. Romeo and Juliet was first performed at The Curtain theatre, in Shoreditch. By an amazing coincidence, my son moved to Shoreditch in 2021, and rented a flat built on the exact spot where The Curtain theatre was built. (Shakespeare and his actors later dismantled it and rebuilt it south of the river Thames, as The Globe).

Top Ten Facts About Verona

1. Verona was a city in Italy, closely allied with Venice. Venice was a military and economic power, due to the strength of her navy. So Verona was well known as wealthy. It also had strong links to the Pope. When I write that Shakespeare made fun of Italians, there was no country of Italy, just an alliance of regions who spoke the same language and had the same cultures, but different rulers.

2. Verona was well known for its churches.

3. It had a very intact Colosseum. You can still visit it today as it is home to the Verona opera - that's how awesome the acoustics are. Some scholars have argued that Shakespeare must have travelled to Italy, because he set so many of his plays there. However, to write about Verona without mentioning the Colosseum, especially in such a violent play, probably implies that he didn't know about it.

4. Elizabethans were fascinated by the Venetians, because of their wealth, success in trade and promotion of art and architecture. Othello was a Venetian general. Shylock was the merchant of Venice. Verona was part of the Venetian republic.

5. Elizabethans knew about Verona from a translation of the 1530 Italian story of star-crossed lovers, Romeo Montecchi and Giulietta Cappelletti. This then became the source for the even more familiar Arthur Brooke poem for the 1560s.

6. Because of the artistic developments in painting and sculpture in Italy, many of the English nobles had travelled to Italy. Some arranged for Italian tutors for their children. Shakespeare's patron, the Earl of Southampton, employed an Italian tutor for himself.

7. Petrarch, the Italian poet and sonnet writer, was immensely popular in England. His poems were written to the fictional 'Laura' who would not return his love. Mercutio references Laura when he makes fun of Romeo's poetry of love: **"Laura to his lady was a kitchen wench (marry, she had a better love to berhyme her)"**. Mercutio hilariously implies that Romeo is partly in love with Rosaline as her name is so easy to rhyme with, making her a convenient subject for his love poetry.

8. Masked balls had become popular in England since the time of Henry VIII. However, they were imported from Venice. Although women were forbidden to perform on stage, in a masked ball they were encouraged to be part of the entertainment. Balls were themed, and because only the wealthy attended, costumes were lavish and extravagant. Women were able to be much more flirtatious and sexually alluring than in their day to day lives, because of the illusion of disguise.

9. Italy was known to be made up of city states, with very different cultures and customs. This makes it easy for the audience to believe that Romeo would be horrified at being banished, not just from Verona, but to an alien city, Mantua.

10. The rivalry between the city states also led Elizabethans to see the Italians as inherently violent. They were also famous for their blood feuds, where families would be enemies across the generations.

Part 3: Themes

Top Ten Themes

1. Fate

Shakespeare uses the conventions of tragedy to explain the lovers' deaths. But Fate alone is not responsible for their deaths, they both contribute through their hubris, arrogantly challenging social convention, God and the warnings from Romeo's dream.

2. Love

Shakespeare juxtaposes the lovers' youthful belief in love with often overwhelming evidence that what they are feeling is simply sexual desire. He asks us to consider the role of love in marriage and the prohibitions on sex before marriage. How far does the patriarchal cult of virginity cause the lovers to rush into marriage?

3. Violence

Violence is a real cause of the tragedy. Verona is beset by the violence of the feud, and this violence is supported by the social convention of masculine honour and duelling. But Shakespeare makes sure to begin the play with humour about sexual violence, implying that male power makes them dangerous to rivals, but also to all women who are, one way or another, abused in the play.

4. Youth

Shakespeare juxtaposes two worlds, the perspective of youth and the adult perspective. Although all the voices of wisdom come from the adult world, especially from Friar Lawrence, so do the various betrayals of Juliet. She is betrayed by her father, who decides to marry her to Paris without her consent, and by her mother who supports this. She is betrayed by the Nurse who protects her position by recommending that Juliet treat Romeo as "dead" and marry Paris bigamously. She is betrayed by the Friar who abandons her in the tomb, having proposed to abandon her in a convent.

And yet the passion of youth often leads to tragedy through impulsive challenges of God, authority and common sense. We empathise with the young for their depth of passion in contrast to the manipulative adult world. By exposing the flaws of each, Shakespeare asks us to reflect on the role of the patriarchal society in driving the causes of the tragedy.

5. Patriarchal Control of Women

From the violent sexual humour that opens the play, to Romeo's bribery to try to have sex with Rosaline, to Lady Capulet's and the Nurses pregnancies at thirteen, to Capulet's marrying off Juliet at thirteen against her will, to Romeo's sexual bravado after marrying, to Mercutio's attack on childbirth, to Capulet's history of infidelity, to Capulet's and Paris's obsession with Juliet's virginity, to the symbolism of Juliet choosing Romeo's dagger to kill herself, this play places the Patriarchal control of women as the root cause of the tragedy. All Juliet's choices are dictated by this control and her desperation to escape it and so attempt to choose her own destiny.

6. Male Honour

A society which arms all its young men could be in a constant state of violence. The code of male honour seeks to formalise this with elaborate etiquette around duels. By raising the stakes, so that death might be a consequence of insult, society tries to create the "gentle" man. Shakespeare attacks this growing fashion in Elizabethan England. So ironically the huge brawls between the Capulets and Montagues have no fatalities, but the duels kill Mercutio, Tybalt and Paris.

Male sexual control of women is the cause of the rebellious decisions Romeo and Juliet make, but it is the code of male honour which glorifies violence that leads to the tragic outcomes.

7. Sex

Shakespeare's plotting and the voices of the Friar, Mercutio, Benvolio and the Nurse all ask us to evaluate how far this love story is actually an illusion driven by sexual desire. Shakespeare makes sure that sex features in every act. The play opens with males joking about rape; Romeo bribes Rosaline to "ope her lap"; Mercutio comments on anal sex as a contraceptive and a way to preserve virginity; Mercutio expresses homosexual desire for Romeo; the Nurse jokes about Juliet learning to fall on her back at three years old; the Friar won't allow Romeo and Juliet to remain alone in case they have sex in church; Romeo and Mercutio joke about prostitution and masturbation; Tybalt taunts Mercutio and Romeo by suggesting they are lovers; Juliet fantasises about sex and orgasm while waiting for Romeo; Capulet reveals a history of infidelity; Capulet tells Paris that death has stolen Juliet's virginity; Paris haunts Juliet's tomb, throwing flowers on the ground as a symbol of Juliet's virginity which has been taken from him.

Shakespeare also uses sex to provide humour, to increase tension between characters and to criticise the patriarchal obsession with virginity as a way of preserving a daughter's moral and financial worth.

8. Catholicism and God

Fate, or "fortune" can't really exist independently of God. The Prologue sets up the tragedy as the only way to **"bury [the] parents' strife"**, as though it were part of God's plan. The Princes words at the end imply that God's judgement has been passed, and tells the parents **"That heaven finds means to kill your joys with love!"** But he adds, **"all are punish'd"** to imply a wider judgement on Verona and the evils of male honour and patriarchal control.

The main instrument of this tragedy is the Friar. This allies Friar Lawrence to God's plan. Without his performance of the marriage, or his mastery of drugs, the lovers' deaths would not have been possible.

But, because Shakespeare's audience will expect an attack on Catholicism, the Friar is also a deeply flawed figure, whose hubris makes him believe he can end the feud and whose cowardice prevents him confessing everything once Romeo is banished. His intelligence, manipulation and duplicity are all used to characterise Catholicism as a false faith, a threat to be resisted despite its apparently virtuous exterior.

9. Masters and Servants

Shakespeare portrays masters as inherently cruel. The servants are frequently the source of comedy, as befits their lowly status, but they are also used to highlight social injustice. Peter mimics the hierarchical nature of his position under Lord Capulet by mocking the musicians for their poverty. Shakespeare the actor-manager seems to be asking why they are worth so little. Romeo is shocked at the apothecary's poverty in a society where people need medicine. Shakespeare is commenting on the new opportunities in England since the dissolution of the monasteries. The Nurse is the butt of men's sexual humour and called a "mumbling fool" and a "gossip" by Capulet. Shakespeare is commenting on the casual and endemic sexism of men. Balthasar is loyal to Romeo, yet he believes that Romeo would actually kill him. Shakespeare is commenting on the power nobles have over their servants.

But Shakespeare also uses the Nurse's betrayal of the Capulets to feed social distrust of servants, who become part of the family, privy to family secrets and, in this instance, keep secrets from their employer.

10. Class and Status

As a businessman, Shakespeare almost existed outside class and status. He sought the patronage of rich noblemen, and finally King James. But his main income was made from all levels of society at his plays, which gave him wealth and independence, no matter the status of his family.

So, we can look at the strict hierarchy in Verona as a criticism of the social system which allows people influence through their birth. For example, had Capulet not been a Lord, there would be no arranged marriage for Juliet. Had Juliet not been rich, Romeo probably wouldn't have wanted to marry her. Had they both been from lower levels in society, they might have courted for years before marrying happily. Had Tybalt and Mercutio not been nobles, there would have been no duels. Looked at this way, we can ask how far Shakespeare is simply describing society, and how far he is portraying it critically, with a view to point out the drawbacks of this class system to the wealthy themselves. Their status seems to bring about their own tragedy.

Shakespeare also uses the convention of prose for characters of low social status and iambic pentameter for characters of noble status. But he also subverts it – when noble characters behave in ways we are meant to criticise, they speak in prose – like Mercutio seeking to fight Tybalt. When lowly characters speak nobly, like the Nurse, they often use iambic pentameter and rhyming couplets. The effect of this is to question the moral value of these social structures which divide society.

It may also be significant that Shakespeare refuses to punish the Nurse with banishment, and refuses to punish the apothecary with death, deviating from Brooke's poem. This results in all the characters who are punished being of noble birth. Perhaps this is a subtle criticism of Elizabethan nobility.

Top Ten Love Quotes

(handwritten: ✓ 20/02/24)

(handwritten annotations: "nonsense", "fool", "tie")

1. Mercutio tells Romeo **"this drivelling love is like a great natural that runs lolling up and down to hide his bauble in a hole"**.

He believes Romeo's love makes him a "natural", a fool, and that Romeo's greatest foolishness is in not realising that he is actually feeling intense lust, not love. He believes Romeo simply wants to "hide his bauble in a hole" which you know is a metaphor for sex.

2. **"Deny thy father and refuse thy name,"** Juliet asks in soliloquy, **"Or if thou wilt not, be but sworn my love, / And I'll no longer be a Capulet"**.

Juliet equates love with rejecting her parents. This is probably because her parents reject the idea of a marriage based on love. They believe noble families operate best when marriage is a patriarchal contract leading to financial and social reward.

3. **"But my true love is grown to such excess / I cannot sum up some of half my wealth"**.

Juliet is so overwhelmed by love that she feels lost for words when trying to describe it. This is the opposite of Romeo at the beginning of the play. Perhaps Shakespeare uses this to signal that Juliet's love is genuine. It could also foreshadow the overwhelming feelings which cause her to commit suicide rather than live without Romeo.

4. **"Alas, that love, whose view is muffled still, / Should without eyes see pathways to his will"**.

Romeo complains that though love is blind, with a "muffled" "view", love can still force you to follow his "pathways" through the strength of his "will". Romeo dramatises blind Cupid as an enemy, desperate to thwart the lover, making him fall in love with an unattainable woman. This is Romeo at the start, where he is still playing the part of a Petrarchan lover as victim of unrequited love. We are supposed to dismiss this as a pose.

(handwritten: "attitude"; "the lover whose undying love is not returned")

5. **"My only love sprung from my only hate,
Too early seen unknown, and known too late!
Prodigious birth of love is it to me
That I must love a loathed enemy."**

(handwritten: "impressive")

Juliet's love is extreme. She believes that a person can have "only" one love in life. Her use of "must" also suggests that it is her fate to "love a loathed enemy". Rather than fleeing from her feelings of love for Romeo, she rushes towards them. This is the "birth of love", he is her "only love" and she "must love" him, no matter what the obstacles. And so she rushes towards her fate, as Shakespeare's tragic heroes do.

6. **"With love's light wings did I o'erperch these walls, For stony limits cannot hold love out"**.

Romeo jokes that he has borrowed Cupid's wings to reach Juliet, but the rest of the metaphor changes this with "o'erperch". This is an allusion to birds. Romeo and Juliet will both compare each other to falcons, who are of course birds of prey, killers. At this moment the "light wings" feel like hope, but the play will end with the "stony limits" of Juliet's tomb. Love will drive them to their

61

deaths, like birds of prey. So, one way to interpret the play is as an attack on love as damages the lovers.

7. My bounty is as boundless as the sea,
My love as deep; the <u>more I give to thee</u>,
The more I have, for both are infinite.

[handwritten annotations: poetic / paired opposites / Love is infinite → unstoppable after death → leads to suicide]

[handwritten margin note: Paired]

Juliet's imagery about love is poetic, but like Romeo's infatuation with Rosaline, filled with cliché. Just as Romeo yoked opposites together, so Juliet links the opposites of giving love away but ending up with more. This idea that love is "infinite" is also what leads to their suicide. It is the unspoken belief that their love will live on infinitely, unstoppably after death. Although this is a deeply poetic view of love, it is also destructive, because it leads directly to their decision to end their lives.

8. "Then love-devouring death do what he dare-/ It is enough I may but call her mine."

[handwritten annotation: eating]

When Romeo tells the Friar about marrying Juliet, he links their marriage directly with death. Although death is personified as an enemy of love, another way to read this is that death gorges on love. This is exactly what Romeo and Juliet do – they gorge on it so that it becomes, like the Friar's warning, "loathsome in its own deliciousness". This imagery, and its timing, suggest that Romeo is attracted to the idea of death from the start.

9. "Therefore love moderately: long love doth so".

Friar Lawrence's advice comes from the adult world. The word "moderately" cannot fit with passion, and to the young lovers would sound like an absence of love. But this adult view also sees passion as destructive, and therefore short. Ultimately, the ending proves the Friar correct, and so the play invites us to moderate our passions. Their passionate deaths also emphasise the passion of the feud, which also dies with the lovers. Linking the passion of their love with the passion which ignited the feud is another way in which the plot supports the Friar's words: moderation is preferable.

10. "O, I have bought the mansion of a love,
  But not possess'd it; and though I am sold,
  Not yet enjoy'd."

Juliet's metaphors about love once she is married are patriarchal. She moves from the fantasy of Romeo becoming a constellation, to the financial realities of a marriage. She has bought a "mansion of a love". Romeo is her home, in the romantic sense, but in the patriarchal sense that is also the fruit of marriage. She and Romeo will at some stage have a mansion, but she will not own Romeo. Instead, in patriarchal terms, she will be his property. That is why she is "sold" as an object to be "enjoy'd". Love, therefore, does not have the power to make them equals.

Top Ten Fate Quotes

1. "From forth the fatal loins of these two foes / A pair of star-crossed lovers take their life"

The Chorus introduces four causes of the tragedy. The first is the parents themselves – they have the "fatal loins", suggesting that they literally give birth to their children's tragedy.

The second cause is the feud caused by the parents, "these two foes".

The third is God, represented by the higher power of the stars, who make them "star-crossed lovers".

And the fourth is the lovers themselves, who choose to "take their life" when, of course, they could simply have decided to live.

2. "The fearful passage of their death-mark'd love,
And the continuance of their parents' rage,
Which, but their children's end, naught could remove"

The Chorus reveals the reason for their fate. First, fate plans for them to fall in love, so their love is "death-mark'd". Their love and subsequent deaths are designed to "remove" "their parents' rage". Fate has had to intervene (or God has had to intervene) because nothing else - "naught" – would work.

3. "I fear too early, for my mind misgives;
Some consequence, yet hanging in the stars,
Shall bitterly begin his fearful date
With this night's revels and expire the term
Of a despised life, clos'd in my breast,"

In Shakespeare's tragedy, unlike Classic Greek, the hero runs towards their own fate rather than desperately trying to avoid it. This makes them more culpable. So, Romeo's dream communicates a tragic fate to him if he goes to "this night's revels".

He realises he will die, "expire the term" because he is living "a despised life". Shakespeare is deliberately ambiguous about whether Romeo himself despises his own life, or if he feels his life is "despised" by Fate or God.

4. "he that hath steerage over my course, direct my sail".

Romeo takes no responsibility for his actions. He deliberately gives up control and allows Fate, God or his friends to dictate his life. His metaphor suggests he won't "steer" himself. The lack of a capital in "he" also implies that Romeo is not truly handing control of his life to God – he wants to believe he is, but in reality "he" is making his own reckless choices.

5. "Affliction is enamoured of thy parts, / And thou art wedded to calamity."

The Friar suggests that Romeo is a victim of Fate, whom he personifies as a lover, called both "affliction" and "calamity". This implies that the marriage itself is the cause of the tragedy. More than this, though, it also personifies Juliet as "calamity". The marriage, remember, was also her idea. When she asks for Romeo to be "cut out in little stars" she becomes the voice of Fate, linking him to death and to the "star-crossed" lover of the Chorus. He is "death-mark'd" by her. The Friar's Christian perspective is always biased to the idea that, since Eve, the woman is more to blame than the man. But the Friar doesn't know about Romeo's warning from Fate, as we do, so we are more inclined to blame him, for likening her to "calamity".

6. "O God, I have an ill-divining soul.
Methinks I see thee now, thou art so low
As one dead in the bottom of a tomb."

Unlike Romeo, Juliet does not get a warning from Fate. Instead, she gets a premonition. Romeo will die, but she also sees him in a vision of her own "tomb". Unlike Romeo, she isn't given the chance to alter this fate. Perhaps we therefore see her as more of a victim than Romeo.

7. "I would the fool were married to her grave!"

Juliet is also the victim of her mother's parenting. We've seen that in Lady Capulet pushing Juliet into a marriage with Paris. Now that Juliet refuses, Lady Capulet's words have the power of a curse: Juliet will die with her husband, and so will be "married to her grave". This curse echoes Mercutio, who called for **"a plague on both your houses"**. This one doesn't quite make my top ten because we don't get the sense that Mercutio causes this plague, whereas we do feel that the patriarchal marriage is a root cause of Juliet's rebellion in marrying Romeo.

8. "Oh, I am fortune's fool".

We could interpret this as the moment that Romeo first realises he is a tragic hero. The hamartia is interesting. What caused him to kill Mercutio? It was not revenge so much as the belief that Juliet's love had made him "effeminate". So, the patriarchal development of male honour, bravery – "valour's steel" - and violence are the cause of his impulsive decision to kill Tybalt.

But it is still Romeo's impulsive decision to make. Even here, he can pull back from his fate. So once again we see him abdicating responsibility, blaming "fortune" when we can see he is simply a "fool".

9. "Then I defy you, stars"

Romeo's hamartia has always been hubris. If we look at the patriarchal view of masculinity which causes him to kill Tybalt, we can see that this is simply male pride. His hubris at the outset was in believing he could defy fate – the "consequence yet hanging in the stars".

Now that he believes Juliet is dead, he also believes he can outwit fate by killing himself. He still sees himself as the hero of his own story, choosing his own destiny. This is ironic because we know this has been Fate's plan all along, and he is not defying the stars at all. Shakespeare also wants us to see that his death is also pointless – Juliet is not in fact dead. Although both deaths serve God's and the Friar's larger purpose, in turning the "enmity" of the feud into "pure love", on a personal level it is a waste of his life.

10. "O, give me thy hand,
One writ with me in sour misfortune's book!
I'll bury thee in a triumphant grave."

Once he has killed Paris, Romeo realises the true level of his foolishness. He now realises that he is not the hero of his own story, just as Paris was not the hero of his. What they both have in common is love of Juliet, or at least a passion for her which makes them prepared to risk dying. Now he understands that Fate has wider plans than he imagined, and that Paris has been written into "misfortune's book" with him.

The book is important. It deliberately harks back to the "golden story" of Paris's life, described by Lady Capulet. Juliet is now going to become his story's "cover" – he is killed because of his passion for her, and he is now dragged by Romeo into a "triumphant grave" in her tomb. His "golden story" is ended with the "pure gold" statues of Romeo and Juliet, to be erected by their parents.

This turning point in Romeo's perception of his role in the tragedy adds a level of nobility to his actions. We might even argue that agreeing to Paris's request to be buried with Juliet is the first time which he has acted in someone else's interests rather than his own.

This nobility allows us to see the waste of his life from another perspective. Rather than see him attracted to the idea of self-destruction from the start, we can argue that he sees his suicide as a sacrifice for Juliet, as part of a wider plan from Fate.

On the other hand, we could still see it as the rash, impulsive act of a young "fool". You choose!

Top Ten Sex Quotes

1. "I will push Montague's men / from the wall and thrust his maids to the wall."

So, Sampson is going to **"thrust [Montague's] maids to the wall",** meaning to rape them. Then "maids" becomes "maidenhead", so woman has become virgin - he is just going to rape the virgins.

The constant sexual references are a challenge. You'll know by now that I think Shakespeare is deeply critical of this masculine bravado. He deliberately starts the play with this violent sexual humour to show what is wrong with patriarchal society in Verona. This helps explain what Romeo is trying to rebel against and why he is partly failing to do so. Juliet too is desperate to escape the kind of male courtship of untrustworthy, sex obsessed lovers and suitors who rely on wealth and power to gain the young bride they want to mould or mar.

2. "My naked weapon is out".

This sexual pun is typical of how Shakespeare uses humour. By linking the violence of the sword and the feud to the penis, he makes the audience laugh at the immature male bravado. But at the same time, he tells his audience that the male attitude to violence and to women are the same idea in different forms - male power used in immature, damaging and dangerous ways.

3. "this driveling love is like a great natural that runs / lolling up and down to hide his bauble in a hole".

Mercutio believes Romeo's belief in love makes him an idiot. The "bauble" was a stick carried by the professional fool or court jester. At its end was a head, so the stick was a miniature version of the jester himself. Mercutio means the "bauble" to represent Romeo's penis, and the "hole" to represent Rosaline's vagina. He means, as usual, that Romeo's feelings of love are simply a misunderstanding of his real desires for sex. That Romeo doesn't realise this makes him seem ridiculous, like the fool.

4. "Oh, I have bought the mansion of a love/ But not possessed it, and, though I am sold, / Not yet enjoyed."

Juliet talks about sex with Romeo, but Romeo never talks about sex with Juliet. We get the sense that she is much more in touch with her feelings and motives, whereas Romeo is continually taken by surprise by his. She sees Romeo as a "mansion of love". The metaphor brings to mind what she will gain from a patriarchal marriage, a palatial home, the title of Lady, security and wealth. In order to gain this, a father literally sells her. She instead chose her own husband, so has "sold" herself. Still, it is a very unromantic view of marriage as a transaction. Although she is looking forward to sex with Romeo, part of the marriage bargain in her view is to bring him enjoyment before her own. She looks forward to being "enjoyed" by him. We can see that she is very clear sighted about the marriage and sex. Her metaphors are much wiser and more original then Romeo's clichés.

5. "Give me my Romeo. And when I shall die, / Take him and cut him out in little stars".

Juliet imagines consummating the marriage. Again, she talks about sex indirectly, in metaphor. She is not literally looking forward to death here - to "die" was Elizabethan slang for orgasm. The idea of a dead hero being commemorated as a constellation comes from Greek myth, for example Hercules and Perseus. Juliet plays with this image, so that when she dies, it is Romeo who will be her hero, presumably for the sexual pleasure he brings her. He will then become a constellation, rather than her, because of course he will also 'die', through the sexual orgasm.

6. "I conjure thee by Rosaline's bright eyes,
By her high forehead and her scarlet lip,
By her fine foot, straight leg, and quivering thigh,
And the demesnes that there adjacent lie".

Mercutio mocks Romeo's conventional, poetic view of love. He invokes Romeo's love poetry, detailing Rosaline's beauty in a formulaic way. Mercutio challenges this by focusing on her sexuality:

Mercutio pictures Romeo imagining Rosaline's "quivering thigh" in response to his sexual advances. He claims Romeo is thinking about the area "adjacent" to the thigh, which Romeo won't even hear named. Mercutio means that Romeo is therefore in denial about his true desires, which are sexual rather than motivated by love.

7. "Now will he sit under a medlar tree
And wish his mistress were that kind of fruit
As maids call medlars when they laugh alone.
O Romeo, that she were, O that she were
An open-arse and thou a poperin pear!"

Although Mercutio also speaks about sex in metaphors, they are sexually explicit. We get the impression that Mercutio is older than Romeo, and is able to imagine what Romeo is actually thinking, rather than what he is saying. According to Mercutio, Romeo is longing for anal sex. This will mean Rosaline could take him as a lover and still remain a virgin, so Romeo can therefore experience sex outside of marriage. After all, if he were really in love, he could seek a marriage and then have no need to preserve Rosaline's virginity. So, Mercutio's metaphors accuse Romeo of not being in love at all. Even more importantly for Mercutio, this metaphor helps him frame Romeo's sexual desire as no different from having anal sex with a man. He is expressing his own desire to have Romeo as a lover, and implying that Romeo would feel the same way if he weren't in the habit of denying his true feelings.

8. "ROMEO: Why, then is my pump well-flowered.
MERCUTIO: Well said: follow me this jest now till thou hast worn out thy pump; that, when the single sole of it is worn, the jest may remain, after the wearing, sole singular."

In this exchange Shakespeare lets us know that Mercutio's perception of Romeo is very accurate. Romeo's sexual metaphor, that his "pump" is "well-flowered" tells Mercutio that he has finally taken Rosaline's virginity. The addition of "well" implies that he has had sex with her repeatedly the previous night of the ball. Mercutio immediately knows this is a lie, simply bravado. This is why, in his metaphor, he implies that Romeo's "pump" has been worn out through his "sole" and "singular" sex - all his sexual pleasure has been masturbating.

This is a very funny put down, because we know Mercutio is right. But, if he is right about this, Shakespeare asks us, is he also right about Romeo mistaking lust for love? We can argue that Romeo has changed, since his true love for Juliet, and after the false and immature love of Rosaline. Mercutio is therefore describing the old Romeo. Perhaps. But then why does Romeo still give in to this bravado when he has married his true love? Perhaps because it is not really all about love, but much more to do with sexual desire.

9. "his heart cleft with the blind bow-boy's butt-shaft".

Mercutio mocks Romeo's love. The alliteration emphasises the "butt". He means that Cupid has managed to pierce Romeo's heart with the blunt end of his arrow. This symbolises how this love is not real, that any woman can make Romeo fall in love with her, because what his is really interested in is sex. The "shaft" is the length of the arrow, and the end which sits on the bowstring is grooved. This is called the "butt" because it is the end, but also because the groove makes it look like buttocks. "Shaft" is also slang for penis. At the very least, Mercutio is again pointing out that Romeo is feeling only lust. But the juxtaposition of imagery describing buttocks and penis is a recurring theme for Mercutio, and it also implies his own sexual desires for Romeo.

10. "O son, the night before thy wedding day
Hath Death lain with thy wife. See, there she lies,
Flower as she was, deflowered by him."

One cause of Romeo and Juliet's tragedy is their passionate sexual desire. This is the only reason for Romeo to enter into such a hasty marriage.

But a wider cause is the patriarchal control of sex. Not only must a woman remain a virgin until she is married, she cannot choose her own husband. Shakespeare wants his audience to feel deeply uncomfortable about this, which is why he gives Capulet these words to describe Juliet. For him, Juliet's role was simply to lose her virginity, selling her sexuality in exchange for a husband of his choosing. Now that Juliet is dead, he doesn't just mourn her as his daughter. He mourns the loss of the sexual exchange with Paris. This is why he describes death as a lover, who has "deflowered" Juliet before her wedding day. This extended metaphor shockingly equates the idea of a woman taking a lover (and not being a virgin) with losing her to death. They appear to be equal tragedies in this patriarchal world. This is what makes the patriarchal society obscene, and why the whole plot of the play attacks it.

Top Ten Death Quotes

The word "death" occurs 75 times in the play!

1. "From forth the fatal loins"

The Prologue describes the parents as "fatal loins". The deliberate suggestion is that the parents are the ultimate cause of their children's deaths. Although the lovers are **"death-mark'd"**, this is connected to their birth – an ironic reversal of the birth mark.

2. "Turn thee Benvolio! look upon thy death."

Tybalt is the first character to mention death. He is the catalyst the tragedy needs – without him, Romeo won't get banished, and the Friar's plan to reveal the marriage and broker peace between the feuding families might work.

Tybalt's words also point to the dangers of the patriarchal support of male honour, which seem to make the deaths of young men inevitable. This is not Fate, but the consequence of socially endorsed behaviours.

3. "Go ask his name. - If he be married, My grave is like to be my wedding bed."

We can almost hear Shakespeare chuckling into his beard at this irony. "If" can mean both whether and when. And when Romeo is married, Juliet's wedding bed becomes her grave. This motif, linking the death to the marriage throughout the play, keeps reinforcing Shakespeare's point that the patriarchal rules around virginity and sex are the root cause of the lovers' deaths.

4. "Come death, Juliet wills it so"

This quotation is one of the many which show Romeo's infatuation with death. It also contains the added irony that Juliet brings his death about when she takes the Friar's drug. We could even argue her "will" caused his death from the moment she insisted on marriage.

5. "Methinks I see thee, now thou art below, As one dead in the bottom of a tomb."

Shakespeare loves his irony. But the image also links death to their marriage, which has only become binding since the lovers consummated it. This suggests that the marriage is the cause of their tragedy. Firstly, Shakespeare does this to continually undermine the idea of Fate, working against the lovers. Secondly, it argues that the tragedy is not caused by a divine fate, but by patriarchal social rules, which demand that a woman must remain a virgin until marriage.

6. "They have made worms meat of me".

Shakespeare gives Mercutio many lines after he has been stabbed with "a scratch". His humour appears both brave and noble. But in this quotation, he wants the audience to see the finality of death. He doesn't look forward to any kind of afterlife, or a benign and caring God. Instead, he points out the sad fact that he is just a body of "meat", and that his fate is to be eaten by the lowliest of creatures, a "worm". Mercutio also blames "they", the two "houses" of Montague and Capulet whom he curses with "a plague". Like Romeo, he denies personal responsibility – after all, he chose to fight Tybalt. It is his fault alone. But his words also reinforce Shakespeare's other message, that the patriarchal society encouraged by the "houses" is the cause of the tragedy.

7. "And, in this rage, with some *great* kinsman's bone / As with a club dash out my desp'rate brains?"

Juliet imagines herself waking up in her tomb, surrounded by her ancestors' bones. The symbolism of this vision suggests that these men will drive her to suicide. She picks the most patriarchal bone she can find, one from a "great kinsman" and uses it to "dash out [her] brains". This strongly implies that she will be driven to suicide by patriarchal men, seeking to control her. It also implies that living as a wife in such a patriarchal marriage is a form of suicide, because it is a giving up on life.

8. "O son, the night before thy wedding day
Hath Death lain with thy wife. See, there she lies,
Flower as she was, deflowered by him."

We keep meeting this quotation. Here let's focus on irony again. Who has literally "lain with" Juliet before her "wedding day" to Paris? Romeo. So ironically, Romeo is the human form "Death" takes.

Personifying death this way also undermines the belief in a Christian afterlife. Only "Death" is waiting when we die. This might simply reflect Capulet's belief, marking him out as a reprehensible character to Shakespeare's Christian audience. Or it may prove part of the message of the play. There is no afterlife for Romeo and Juliet, in which love triumphs over death. There is only "Death". Or you may decide that the ending instead reveals God's plan – the feud is over, order is restored, and God will accept them into heaven.

9. "That unsubstantial Death is amorous,
And that the lean abhorred monster keeps
Thee here in dark to be his paramour?"

Romeo's metaphor of death as a lover who has imprisoned Juliet "in dark" is different to Capulet who saw death as a mirror image of patriarchal man, interested in possession. He does not blame "Death" for falling love with Juliet, and does not imagine death to be motivated by any sort of status at having so young, or rich a lover. This might imply that Romeo truly thinks of Juliet in loving terms, without any consideration of her status as the daughter of "rich Capulet". We might even argue that he is no longer fixated on her body, that "amorous" implies a deeper connection than sex. However, the word "paramour" means an illicit lover – illicit because she would be already married. So, at the end of the image, Romeo is still imagining sex with Juliet, even after death. If we choose, we can still argue that his love is dominated by sexual passion.

10. "O happy dagger, / This is thy sheath. There rust and let me die."

Juliet kills herself symbolically with Romeo's dagger. Shakespeare dramatises the idea that Romeo is responsible for her death, as he sets the whole tragedy in motion. He has also taken the final step, in killing himself, which leads to Juliet's tragic death. Finally, he has chosen that Juliet must use the dagger instead of Romeo's poison. This allows her death to become a sexual metaphor for their sexual union: Romeo's "dagger" enters her "sheath", her body, to kill her. Although this implies a loving union in death, it also points to sexual passion as the main attraction between the young lovers.

Top Ten Symbols

1. Light/Dark, Black/White Imagery

The play is full of light and dark imagery. Partly this is because all plays took place in daylight in a theatre without a roof. Night time scenes demanded torch light and characters commenting on the dark to help set the context for an audience standing or sitting in sunlight.

But Shakespeare often uses it to provide a tragic contrast, or to hint at the lover's coming deaths.

So, when Capulet tells Paris that the ball will be filled with **"Earth-treading stars that make dark heaven light"**, we pick up the echo of **"star-crossed lovers"**. It is not just the huge number of torches and candles he is describing, but symbolically it is Fate drawing ever closer to the "Earth", seeking out Romeo and Juliet.

When Benvolio describes Romeo: **"Blind is his love, and best befits the dark"**, we pick up on the symbolism. Romeo is also blind to his fate, and his fate is "the dark" of death.

Juliet reveals her love for Romeo in soliloquy, not knowing he can hear her. She asks:
therefore pardon me,
And not impute this yielding to light love,
Which the dark night hath so discovered.

The contrast between her "light love" and "dark night" symbolically suggests impending death. This is emphasised by using "discovered" instead of revealed or uncovered. Her verb choice suggests the darkness has been looking for her love, like a hunter. Now Fate has found them.

Romeo's language also plays with this symbolism when he speaks about his banishment. Because he must be gone before daylight, he observes: **"More light and light, more dark and dark our woes"**. This contrast accentuates that each coming day brings them closer to the darkness of their fate.

When at last their fate arrives, Romeo's imagery loses this contrast, light is left behind and he focuses only on darkness: **"And that the lean abhorred monster keeps/ Thee here in dark to be his paramour?"**

It is noticeable that, unlike Capulet and Paris, Romeo feels no jealousy that death is Juliet's lover. He will join them both.

2. Crow, Swan

The light and dark imagery is also introduced by Benvolio when he introduces Romeo to his fate. It is his idea, after all, that Romeo should attend the Capulet ball: **"Compare her face with some that I shall show, / And I will make thee think thy swan a crow."** The darkness of the crow again reminds us of death.

Benvolio also criticises the idea of dressing a boy up as Cupid as a way to introduce them to the ball. He describes this Cupid as **"Scaring the ladies like a crow-keeper"**. Symbolically, this links love, through Cupid, to death, through "crow". So, Benvolio's language propels Romeo closer to death as he introduces him to his love.

Romeo picks up on the same imagery when he falls in love with Juliet at first sight: **"So shows a snowy dove trooping with crows"**. He has internalised the contrast between black and white, and Benvolio's symbolism of the crow. It is interesting that he changes "swan", which would have alliterated with the sibilance of "shows a snowy", in preference for "dove" which, as Mercutio tells us, is a love poet's cliché. Perhaps he does this because a "dove" is a very similar shape to a "crow", much smaller than a "swan". Perhaps this implies Romeo is also attracted to Juliet's youth, unlike the probably older Rosaline who saw Romeo's seduction as Cupid's "childish bow".

3. Dove

Despite her youth, the "dove" is also a symbol of Juliet's independence. Perhaps for this reason the Nurse is very specific about where she was when she "wean'd" Juliet, smearing her nipple with "wormwood" to make it taste bitter. She was **"Sitting in the sun under the dovehouse wall"**. The dovehouse gives the birds the illusion of freedom – they can always fly away. But they return for food, until one day they are taken, killed, and served as food themselves. So, the dove becomes not just a symbol of love, but also death. It is also a symbol for the life of a wife in this society.

Mercutio mocks the link between "love" and "dove" in unimaginative lovers' poetry: **"Cry but 'Ah me!' Pronounce but Love and dove"**. Interestingly, it is Juliet who makes this link, when she has married Romeo, but is waiting to consummate the marriage: **"Therefore do nimble-pinion'd doves draw love, / And therefore hath the wind-swift Cupid wings."** This use of "dove" and "love" together undermines our faith in her love. It deliberately calls it into question and suggests that perhaps Juliet's sexual passion has made her mistake her feelings for love.

4. Stars

Stars are always a symbol of Fate in the play because Shakespeare anchors us to that image in the Prologue, when we find **"A pair of star-cross'd lovers take their life"**.

Capulet links his ball to fate, when he describes the lighting as **"Earth-treading stars that make dark heaven light"**. This irony implies that by taking Paris and his marriage proposal to the ball, Capulet himself is provoking the fate which will kill Juliet.

Shakespeare makes sure Romeo receives a direct warning, rather than an ironic one. He wants us to know that Romeo made a conscious decision to challenge and defy fate: **"I fear too early: for my mind misgives/ Some consequence yet hanging in the stars"**.

When he sees Juliet on her balcony, Romeo's flattery also links Juliet to her fate through imagery of the stars: **"The brightness of her cheek would shame those stars"**. This language also includes a symbolic challenge to fate, because he imagines the "stars" will feel shame at the sight of Juliet.

Juliet uses the same imagery when she imagines Romeo, as the hero of her love, been made into a constellation: **"Take him and cut him out in little stars"**. The irony of this is that she invites Fate to do this "when I die", which is exactly what happens. When he kills himself because of her simulated death she ironically causes his tragic death, and we can argue these very words initiate that fate.

When Romeo hears that Juliet is dead, he imagines that the fate he foresaw in his dream has now been realised. He believes that when he kills himself, this will be a challenge to Fate: **"Is it even so? Then I defy you, stars!"** Perhaps he thinks that when the Prince banished him instead of executing him, that Fate had intervened to keep him alive. Or perhaps he believes that Fate planned to kill him some other way, and he chooses to kill himself. The dramatic irony we know is that both lovers are "star-crossed" and Fate requires them both to die: he is doing exactly what fate requires.

But by the time he has killed Paris, he has rethought this. He realises his role as a tragic hero, and that his own death is part of his fate. So he returns one last time to the imagery of "stars" as fate: **"O, here/ Will I set up my everlasting rest; / And shake the yoke of inauspicious stars".**

He imagines that his "inauspicious" luck will end in death. In Christian doctrine, suicide was seen as a sin, and he would be buried in unconsecrated ground. His soul would not go to heaven. However, Shakespeare has crafted the play, particularly with the intervention of the Friar and the Prologue, with the Christian symbolism of the pomegranate tree outside Juliet's window, to suggest that the lovers' deaths are part of God's plan to end the feud. The Elizabethans might well suppose their souls will find heaven, despite their suicides. Or, they might see it as another example of their youthful arrogance.

5. Poison

Shakespeare uses poison to explore the nature of good and evil. In particular, he points out that the border between them is porous. A poison is not simply poison, but in the right dose is also medicine. He uses it to explore the idea of balance, of not giving in to extremes. He introduces poison and balance through the carefully crafted rhyming couplets of the Friar:

Within the infant rind of this weak flower
Poison hath residence, and medicine power

From this perspective love itself is a medicine which, in the excess of Romeo and Juliet's passion, is a poison.

Benvolio first notices this when he calls love an "infection" of the "eye": **"Take thou some new infection to thy eye. / And the rank poison of the old will die."**

When Juliet hears the Nurse's grief about Tybalt's death, without mentioning the victim's name, she assumes Romeo is dead. Astonishingly, she does not assume Romeo has been killed in the feud, but instead immediately leaps to the idea of suicide:

Hath Romeo slain himself? Say thou but Ay,
And that bare vowel I shall poison more
Than the death-darting eye of cockatrice.

In metaphor, her mind leaps to "poison", as Shakespeare hints that her emotions are out of balance because their love is too intense. He also hints that this makes both lovers predisposed to self-destruction.

The next reference to poison occurs with Lady Capulet's plans to have "vengeance" and hire an assassin to kill Romeo, who **"Shall give him such an unaccustom'd dram"** of poison that he will die. The advantage of poison is that it is often an unseen cause, and perhaps can't be traced back to the Capulets.

Through irony, this also works as an appeal to Fate. It is exactly how Romeo does die. This death then causes Juliet's death, a clear signal that Shakespeare wants us to blame the Capulet parents.

When Romeo finally dies he personifies poison as a guide: **"Come, bitter conduct, come, unsavoury guide. / Thou desperate pilot, now at once run on/ The dashing rocks thy seasick, weary bark. Here's to my love! (drinks the poison)."** He drinks to Juliet, but the secondary meaning is that poison will be the "pilot" who will guide him to Juliet. We feel the romance of this gesture, even though we might doubt this happy afterlife awaits them.

6. Trees

Where underneath the grove of sycamore
That westward rooteth from this city side,
So early walking did I see your son.

Shakespeare uses trees symbolically. The sycamore is normally symbolic of strength and protection. However, we can't help wonder if the sound of the word is important, suggesting that Romeo is suffering from 'more sickness', through his belief in love.

MERCUTIO: Now will he sit under a medlar tree, / And wish his mistress were that kind of fruit

We've explored the sexual meanings of this tree and its fruits. Leaving Mercutio's homosexual desires aside, there is a key social point here. If you want to enjoy sexual activity outside of marriage and avoid becoming pregnant or causing a pregnancy, this is the only version of safe sex available.

Mercutio uses it to undermine Romeo's claims of love, and replace them with sexual desire. He implies Romeo's desire is so great, that he will entertain any sexual practice, no matter how socially unacceptable it might be.

When Romeo woos Juliet at her balcony, Shakespeare makes him comment on the trees:

Lady, by yonder blessed moon I vow,
That tips with silver all these fruit-tree tops,

Perhaps the "fruit-tree" is an echo of Eden, and the Fall through Eve's temptation. It hints at the idea that they are about to commit a sin by marrying.

Shakespeare also places a "pomegranate tree" outside Juliet's window: **"Nightly she sings on yond pomegranate tree."** This was used in Elizabethan art as a symbol of fertility, but also of eternal life, through belief in Jesus. This therefore implies God's blessing over the marriage, despite the fact that it will lead to tragedy. Fate is therefore also God's will, rather than simple punishment for hubris.

Shakespeare places yew trees in the graveyard. We could argue that this is not significant, as yew trees are routinely planted in graveyards, as they are now. Paris instructs his page: **"Under yond yew tree lay thee all along"** and Balthasar **"did sleep under this yew tree here"**.

On the other hand, we do know that Shakespeare focused on their poisonous nature a decade later when he wrote Macbeth. Here the witches use yew as a poisonous ingredient in their potion, **"slips of yew silvered in the moon's eclipse"**. The tree's symbolic link with death and poison works perfectly to prepare us for the lovers' tragic ending.

7. Birds of Prey

NURSE: Romeo's a dishclout to him. An eagle, madam, / Hath not so green, so quick, so fair an eye/ As Paris hath.

The Nurse compares Paris to Romeo, and picks on the "eagle". This is the king of birds of prey. He comes from a richer and more noble family than Romeo. This image also makes him appear older than Romeo, implied by the eagle's greater size compared to the falcon.

JULIET: Hist! Romeo, hist! O for a falconer's voice/ To lure this tassel-gentle back again.

Juliet imagines herself in control of Romeo as the falconer controls the falcon, which offers us a clue at how much her marriage is motivated by her need for independence. The falcon she imagines is a "tassel-gentle", the Peregrine, the noblest of falcons. This attributes both great status and gentleness to Romeo, which are other reasons she might love him.

JULIET: Romeo.
ROMEO: My nyas?

Romeo's metaphor compares Juliet to a "nyas", a young falcon which is being trained. He uses it as a term of affection, but it unsettles us in a number of ways. Firstly, he sees himself as the falconer, controlling Juliet. We therefore see that each believes themselves to be in control of the other, which is a clue their love is untested and perhaps doomed to conflict. Secondly, "nyas" refers to Juliet's young age. Part of the attraction of her youth might be that Romeo believes he can train her, mould her to his will. In patriarchal terms, it also implies that part of this training will be sexual – her role will be to satisfy him, rather than see sex as an equal partnership.

BENVOLIO: We'll have no Cupid hoodwink'd with a scarf

This image is another of Shakespeare's prophetic uses of irony. To "hoodwink" a falcon is to keep it calm and awaiting instruction in the hunt. By not hoodwinking Cupid, Benvolio implies that love will have free reign to hunt where it wants. It implies a bird of prey which is out of control. And at the ball, love does hunt Romeo and Juliet, and it does act as a bird of prey, because we can argue their love does kill them.

8. Bones

MERCUTIO: The collars, of the moonshine's watery beams; / Her whip of cricket's bone; the lash, of film

Even though Mercutio's description of Queen Mab is fanciful at the beginning, it is still full of violence. Her whip is made out of the bones of a dead cricket, perhaps killed for the purpose, and it is still a "whip", to inflict pain.

Mercutio says of Tybalt: **that we should be thus afflicted with these strange flies, these fashion-mongers, these pardon-me's, who stand so much on the new form that they cannot sit at ease on the old bench? O their bones, their bones!**

While he mocks Tybalt for his obsession with etiquette, manners and male honour, the choice of "bones" also reminds us of his mortality. (Juliet will emphasise this later in her dream about waking in the tomb amongst her family's bones – Tybalt will be lying near her in the same vault).

NURSE: I am aweary, give me leave awhile;
Fie, how my bones ache! What a jaunt have I had!

JULIET: I would thou hadst my bones, and I thy news:

Shakespeare enjoys the irony again. Juliet's wish that the Nurse should have her bones is made as joke, and literally means that she would give up her young bones in order to get the news about marriage to Romeo from the Nurse. But it also, metaphorically, comes to pass. When Juliet dies, the Nurse is left with Juliet's bones.

JULIET: Chain me with roaring bears;
Or hide me nightly in a charnel-house,
O'er-cover'd quite with dead men's rattling bones,
With reeky shanks and yellow chapless skulls.

This imagery reveals her extreme emotions, but Juliet is also fixated on death, and in particular the "charnel-house" which is her family vault. This foreshadows and explains her eagerness to commit suicide when Romeo is dead, because she has already imagined herself vividly among the dead.

She imagines herself waking from her "shrunk death" in her family tomb, snapping off part of a skeleton and turning mad: **"with some great kinsman's bone, / As with a club, dash out my desperate brains?"**

Once again it reveals her obsession with death and suicide. However, it is also a "kinsman's bone", not that of a female ancestor. This choice implies that it is the male, patriarchal control, which is driving her to this madness and suicide. In this way, Shakespeare attacks that patriarchal control in his own society.

9. Fish

GREGORY: 'Tis well thou art not fish; if thou hadst, thou hadst been poor John. Draw thy tool; here comes of the house of Montagues.

Fish are used as sexual symbols in Elizabethan culture and at the beginning of the play. "poor John" was the cheapest kind of fish you could by. It was so dried that it was hard as wood, from tail to head. Gregory is carrying on Sampson's joke about standing, and suggesting that Sampson himself would have an erection which was hard, but cheap and ugly like the fish. Because "fish" also referred to prostitutes, he is also suggesting that this is why he has a fishy erection – he is so ugly, he has to pay for sex.

Lady Capulet: "The fish lives in the sea, and 'tis much pride / For fair without the fair within to hide." This is a bit of tongue twister and a riddle. On the one hand, Juliet's mother suggests that there are some excellent fish to be caught in the sea, for example Paris. But on the other hand, fish was slang for vagina. And the image of hiding something fair within something fair reminds us of her later metaphor of Juliet being the golden cover to Paris's golden book. In this interpretation Juliet is the fair fish who will hide the fair Paris within her. (Without here means outside, the opposite of within).

MERCUTIO: Without his roe, like a dried herring. O flesh, flesh, how art thou fishified!

"Roe" are fish eggs. Firstly, Mercutio means Romeo has expended all his eggs, like a herring which has had all the eggs removed. This metaphor suggests that Romeo has no sperm left, having been drained by a night time of sex. We know what fish represent, so Mercutio is suggesting that Romeo has been having so much sex that he either smells of fish, or has become part fish. This is said to Benvolio. Once Romeo arrives and begins boasting about deflowering his virgin lover, Mercutio claims not to believe him.

10. Gold

Romeo uses gold to bribe Rosaline: **"Nor ope her lap to saint-seducing gold"**. First, he confesses that he has given her gifts of gold in the hope that this would literally get her to "ope her lap" to him. Despite all his protestations about love, it shows that he links the power of wealth with sex. This is the same impulse that leads Paris to assume that Juliet must be in love with him.

Secondly, he sees "gold" as an instrument of corruption. It is so powerful that it would even seduce a "saint". He returns to this image when he tells the apothecary how evil he considers money is: **"There is thy gold- worse poison to men's souls"**. It may be that after falling in love with Juliet, he realises that his own prior behaviour with Rosaline was morally corrupt.

When Lady Capulet asks Juliet to consider marrying Paris, she describes Juliet as a wife:

"That in gold clasps locks in the golden story;
So shall you share all that he doth possess,
By having him making yourself no less."

She tries to dress up the patriarchal exploitation of Juliet almost as its opposite, a meeting of equals. She is the "gold" cover to Paris's "golden story". But this is an illusion. Yes, both are golden, but she is only the superficial cover, the eye candy, the proof of his power and wealth, being able to attract such a young, beautiful and wealthy bride. He, however, not only benefits from that, but the freedom of being able to write and live his own "golden story". This metaphor clearly shows the agency, independence and free well rich men have in comparison to their wives.

Her promise that Juliet will be "no less" than him, because she will possess "him" is a disingenuous lie. The truth is that she will only "share all that he doth possess" in terms of material things – but she will never possess her husband's freedoms and status as an individual.

Shakespeare uses Lady Capulet's imagery to show how patriarchal society has made her believe these lies, and to highlight the injustice to his audience.

———————————————

When Benvolio first talks about Romeo, to Lady Montague, he explains:

"Madam, an hour before the worshipp'd sun
Peer'd forth the golden window of the east,
A troubled mind drave me to walk abroad"

Here Benvolio uses "golden" to contrast the beauty of the dawn and his own "troubled mind". Shakespeare gives us an insight into the teenage brain. Romeo is troubled because he is not loved by Rosaline. Benvolio's troubles are unspecified. They are probably introduced to show us that this state of unease and lack of sleep is normal for all teenagers, even those as level headed as Benvolio.

The Friar talks about Romeo's youth nostalgically, painting a picture of youth as a time without real worries or cares:

"But where unbruised youth with unstuff'd brain
Doth couch his limbs, there golden sleep doth reign."

Shakespeare uses this ironically. Romeo has not had "golden sleep" since Rosaline began to reject him. And last night he had no sleep at all, spending it at the ball and in Juliet's garden. This portrays the Friar as lacking in understanding of Romeo and perhaps the essence of being a teenager. We could make a strong case for the whole play being about the problem of adults not understanding the inner lives of teenagers.

Romeo again turns against the idea of gold, linking it to harm. When he complains that banishment is a punishment as terrible as death, he tells the Friar:

"Calling death banished,
Thou cutt'st my head off with a golden axe,
And smilest upon the stroke that murders me."

This scene, you remember, reveals Romeo at his most immature, like a toddler. Although we sympathise with his feelings, we can't really empathise with them – his actions and feelings, weeping on the ground, are ridiculous. Shakespeare and the Friar see the banishment as "golden", a wonderful gift. Romeo is only able to see gold as an object of corruption, so banishment simply tries to hide its true nature as an "axe", an instrument of death. Perhaps Shakespeare, the financially astute business man of wealth, is trying to show that this dismissal of gold is also childish.

Shakespeare presents the case for gold when he introduces the economic hardship of the musicians. Peter tells the musicians at the funeral that he will choose the name of the song they should sing: **"I will say for you. It is 'music with her silver sound' because musicians have no gold for sounding."**

Peter makes the musicians lack of "gold", their poverty, a subject of his jokes and taunting. Shakespeare is probably pointing out the injustices of society, which rewards its creative performers so poorly. It is no coincidence that he moved from being an actor, to writing his own plays, to running his own theatre company, to owning his own theatre. Performers, he suggests, are terribly undervalued.

The final image of the play is also of gold.

"MONTAGUE: But I can give thee more,
For I will raise her statue in pure gold,
That whiles Verona by that name is known,
There shall no figure at such rate be set
As that of true and faithful Juliet."

The statue of Juliet will represent her worth, her "rate". This is not based on her beauty, but her loyalty to her husband. Montague sees her suicide as a "true" and "faithful" act, staying loyal to her husband Romeo even after he has died.

This is a worrying image. It implies Juliet made the right decision in killing herself. It implies that the most important aspect of a wife's identity is that she is always "faithful" in a society, as Capulet has shown us, where rich men do not feel the need to be "true" themselves.

In the end, the "gold" statue is simply a symbol for how patriarchal society values daughters – they are commodities, to be exchanged like gold is, for power and status.

Part 4: Form and Structure

Top Ten Examples of Impulsiveness and Hubris

Hubris was the name given for excessive pride. The tragic hero will often feel hubris and therefore believe they can escape fate, or outwit the gods. This causes them to act impulsively.

We can argue that the root cause of all the impulsiveness in the play is hubris.

For example, Romeo and Juliet both believe they can marry their families' enemy in secret, without consequences. Romeo believes he can gate-crash Capulet's ball, and outwit fate, "Some consequence yet hanging in the stars". Perhaps we can argue that their faith in love is also hubris. Love is never enough.

We could argue that every key decision in the play is impulsive. Here are some of them, with the Top Ten involving hubris in bold.

1. Romeo choosing to go to the ball, even though his dreams have warned him against it: "I fear too early, for my mind misgives/ Some consequence yet hanging in the stars/ Shall bitterly begin his fearful date."

2. Mercutio inviting Romeo to the Capulet's ball when his uncle, the Prince, has already threatened Capulet and Montague with execution if there is another fight.

3. The Friar's decision to marry the lovers in order to bring the families together.

4. The Nurse's decision to aid Juliet in going against her parents, the Nurse's employers.

5. Mercutio fighting Tybalt because Romeo won't, but believing he will easily defeat Tybalt.

6. Tybalt's attack on Mercutio when he is defenceless because of Romeo's intervention.

7. Romeo's intervention which leads to Mercutio being killed.

8. Romeo killing Tybalt.

9. Capulet bringing forward the plan to marry Juliet and Paris.

10. Juliet's mother agreeing to the marriage, despite the hint that she regretted marrying so young herself: **"And too soon marred are those so early made"** into mothers.

11. The Nurse who risks Juliet's soul going to hell by advising her to marry Paris when she is already married.

12. The Friar believing the secret marriage can end the feud.

13. Juliet's threat of suicide unless the Friar helps her.

14. The Friar risking Juliet's death with the poison to make her appear dead. Risking deceiving the Capulets.

15. Paris guarding Juliet's tomb and threatening Romeo.

16. The apothecary selling Romeo poison.

17. Romeo committing suicide rather than live without Juliet.

18. The Friar leaving Juliet alone with Romeo's corpse.

19. Juliet committing suicide rather than live without Romeo.

Top Ten Structural Questions

1. Why does he begin with Sampson and Gregory and sex before the fight?

To show the link between sexual oppression of women and violence in society and men. Our laughter encourages us to realise that society has simply accepted this, and Shakespeare's frequent linking of sex and violence challenge us to ask if society needs to change its treatment of women and its celebration of male honour.

2. Why is Rosaline a Capulet?

It reveals Romeo's rebellious nature and his opposition to the feud. It presents him as a risk taker with a predisposition to fall in love with another Capulet by gate crashing a ball which will be filled with Capulet girls and women.

3. Why does Mercutio speak the Queen Mab speech?

At the level of box office, this is a star turn for a favourite actor. It is a piece of fantasy in which the actor can truly show off his craft (we don't know who this would have been). Thematically, his speech is all about the corruption of desires. It therefore suggests that Romeo's dream of death if he goes to the ball is actually a desire for death. It builds to a climax as Queen Mab forces women to "bear" through sex. So, Mercutio's greatest anger is aimed at the dangers of pregnancy, which is particularly relevant given that Lady Capulet and the Nurse both gave birth at thirteen and, if she had lived, Juliet would also have given birth at fourteen or fifteen. This is an attack on early marriage.

4. Why does the Friar speak in rhyming couplets so often?

Although in the end the Friar turns out to be a manipulative coward, he does try to marry the lovers for noble, selfless reasons. His couplets reflect the seriousness of his thought, the desire to keep things in balance (which is what a rhyme does) and also suggest that he is full of wisdom.

5. Why does Tybalt spot Romeo at the ball, rather than simply start another brawl?

In Brooke's poem, Tybalt isn't present at the ball. Spotting Romeo there accentuates Romeo's risk taking. It also dramatises the conflict between Tybalt's desire to escalate the feud and Capulet's desire to win by other means – forging a powerful alliance with Paris. It is the moment which causes Tybalt to want to kill Romeo specifically, rather than fight Montagues in general. In this way, Shakespeare shows that fate is not simply acting on innocent characters. He keeps reminding us that each character who dies brings on their own deaths through hubris, challenging God, the social order, or the warnings of Fate.

6. Why does Juliet suggest marriage before Romeo does?

This stays true to the source poem, where Juliet takes the lead. In the play it also shows us how Juliet is forced into marriage as the only way to have any sexual experience. The speed she suggests shows how desperate she is to escape the kind of marriage her parents have had, where Lady Capulet's father chose a much older husband for her. She is desperate to marry someone she loves rather than someone chosen for her.

7. Why does Shakespeare include the musicians not wanting to play for the funeral procession?

This scene was intended to be very comic, and Peter was played by Shakespeare's company's most famous comic, Will Kemp. He was also famous as a dancer, so he may have required musicians for his dancing too. However, the musicians' refusal to play is the only time a male character is forced to do something they don't want to. This examines the role of the poor, who are forced to perform acts about which they feel uncomfortable. Either they obey, or face further poverty. We might also draw a comparison between their predicament and the role of women and Juliet in particular – in order to get financial security, they must be sold off to a rich husband.

8. Why does Paris fight Romeo and why does Romeo agree to bring his body into the vault near Juliet?

Paris believes that Romeo plans to mutilate the dead bodies of Tybalt and Juliet. This is entirely logical. What is less logical is why he is outside Juliet's tomb in the first place. It is because he is still obsessed with the "flower" of her virginity, and jealous that death has been her "paramour".

Romeo realises that Paris is driven to fight him by Fate. He realises that by "misfortune" he doesn't know that Juliet was already married to Romeo. Because Romeo sees himself as "fortune's fool", he takes pity on Paris as a fellow victim of Fate. Because he sees himself as a tragic hero, he is willing to see Paris in the same light, and so gives him "a triumphant grave".

9. Why does the Friar not stay by Juliet's side?

If he did, he could prevent Juliet's suicide, which would prevent the full tragedy. It also allows Shakespeare to present him as a coward. His offer to "dispose" of Juliet in a convent may also contribute to her desperation. These details are both intended to discredit the Catholic church. Perhaps only the most committed anti-Catholic would suggest that the Friar's solution was intended to push her towards desperation and suicide.

10. Why does Shakespeare stop Juliet drinking poison but force her to use Romeo's dagger?

Women would stereotypically choose poison rather than a dagger; think of Cleopatra. But it isn't just Juliet's death which is important to the tragedy, it is also what causes Juliet's tragedy which matters. By choosing Romeo's dagger, Shakespeare signals that Romeo is a significant cause. He chose to ignore Fate's warning and went to the ball. But the dagger is also phallic, deliberately so when Juliet describes it as "happy" to enter her as her body becomes its "sheath". On the one hand this suggests the sexual basis of their love. On the other it suggests that she believes there will be some romantic union with Romeo in their deaths. But finally, it suggests that sexual desire, and how it is controlled in this patriarchal society, was also the main cause of their tragedy.

Top Ten Facts About Iambic Pentameter and Free Verse

1. In iambic pentameter, each line should be ten syllables long.

2. The iamb is two syllables paired together. So, the line is made up of pairs of syllables. Annoyingly the iamb is more commonly known as a foot.

3. There are five of these pairs (iambs) in the line. This is why it is called pentameter, because the Greek word for five was penta. So the line is five feet long (but still fits on a page!) I know, an iambic pentameter joke with which you can amaze your friends. Except that is also how we actually describe the line, because an iamb is also a foot. It's annoying.

4. The two syllables in the iamb or foot have a rhythm. This is the meter. The rule is the first syllable is unstressed (or not emphasised when you speak it) and the second syllable is stressed (or emphasised when you speak it).

> For example (the stressed syllables in bold):
>
> O, **she** doth **teach** the **tor**ches **to** burn **bright**!
>
> It **seems** she **hangs** up**on** the **cheek** of **night**

This helps emphasise "she", as Romeo is comparing her to all the other ladies dancing (and to his previous standard of beauty, Rosaline). We can also see how it helps emphasise the alliteration. If the stress had been on "burn" rather than "bright" the feeling would be slightly negative rather than positive. Instead Shakespeare introduces the negative reference to death (because it is a tragedy) quite cautiously. We see this with how he doesn't just say she "hangs", but emphasises "seems" first. (Yes, he is likening her to an earring hanging, but of course the word also invites the association of death by hanging).

5. This is an easy way to get a top grade – notice something about the words that are emphasised by the iambic pentameter, and explain why Shakespeare is emphasising it.

6. Shakespeare also makes a big deal of characters losing control of their iambic pentameter. It suggests something is wrong. For example, the quotation above continues:

> **As a rich jewel in an Ethiop's ear;**
> **Beauty too rich for use, for earth too dear!**

Try reading that out loud. The beginnings just don't work. Romeo would have to say: "**As** a **rich jew**el" for it to sound like speech. Similarly, he would need to emphasise the first syllable of beauty, so that line would start: **Beau**ty **too rich** for **use**. When the syllables have this opposite pattern – stressed followed by unstressed – it is called a spondee, rather than an iamb.

Ok, so what? Well, changing the iambic pentameter always shows something is wrong. What is wrong here? This is the moment he falls in love, and the love is wrong. It is the start of the tragedy. So, grade 9 analysis you can use in any essay about love, or Romeo or Juliet, or tragedy, or...

Remember the Friar telling Romeo off: **"Oh, she knew well / Thy love did read by rote, that could not spell"**. The iamb tells us the emphasis must be on "she". This means the Friar is contrasting what Rosaline "knew" to Juliet's ignorance. What else can you spot?

7. Normally, characters in Shakespeare's plays only get rhyming couplets for really important moments, and to signal the end of a scene. This is very different in Romeo and Juliet, where couplets are everywhere. Samuel Taylor Coleridge argued this made the play more like a poem about love.

Remember when Romeo first talks to Friar Lawrence, the Friar speaks entirely in rhyming couplets. The world made perfect sense to him then, and everything was harmonious, in balance. Now that he has agreed to marry them, the world has become disordered. Now he rarely rhymes because he is out of balance.

8. The opposite of verse (which has a predictable meter) is prose. We might have all sorts of rhythms (meters) in our pose – the way we write or talk – but it is not predictable, because it doesn't have a pattern. This makes it prose.

9. Shakespeare gives prose to his characters who have low social status. When he changes that it is a big deal. So, when Mercutio and Tybalt both use prose it is a sign that they are losing control of their status as gentlemen, giving in to violence and disrespect. Shakespeare does this also to show that fate is not just an outside force (unlike Greek tragedy) it is something the characters themselves all bring on (not just the tragic hero).

10. When characters share the iambic pentameter (because each person speaks fewer than ten syllables):

> **PARIS: That "may be" must be, love, on Thursday next**
> **JULIET: What must be shall be.**
> **FRIAR LAWRENCE: That's a certain text.**

It is very unusual for Shakespeare to share the iambic pentameter between three characters. Even more unusual, they share a rhyming couplet. Usually couplets emphasise an ending of a scene. Here the ending hinted at is Fate - "What must be shall be." Dramatic irony means that Paris interprets this as Juliet's commitment to marry him on Thursday, whereas she means that she intends to kill herself.

Free Verse in Shakespeare's plays are the lines with a meter – so anything that isn't prose – and which does not rhyme.

Top Ten Features of Greek Tragedy

1. Unities

Tragedies try to compress time and space. The Unity of Time states that the action should take place in a single day of twenty-four hours. Shakespeare takes the 9-month period of Brooke's poem and reduces it to 5 days.

The Unity of Place states that the action has to take place in one setting. Shakespeare nearly manages that, with just a few scenes of Act Five set in Mantua.

The Unity of Action stated that there should only be one main action in the play. Aristotle defined this to mean that any action which could be removed without changing the course of the play should be removed. So, we might argue that the scenes where servants prepare the ball, or Peter asks the musicians to play fail this test. The useful way to look at this is to realise Shakespeare knew he was breaking the rules of Classical Tragedy to do this, so valued what these scenes were trying to achieve. The first is a nifty bit of scene changing. The second is the element of comedy Shakespeare uses as catharsis, and social commentary which he weaves throughout the play.

2. Chorus

In Greek Tragedy, the Chorus was a group of actors, speaking in unison, commenting on the tragedy and how the audience should react. In Elizabethan plays the Chorus was a single actor, dressed in black, breaking the fourth wall to remind us that we are watching a construct, to admire the actors and the playwright.

3. Hubris

In Greek tragedy, the gods punish the tragic hero for his hubris. Hubris is a form of arrogance that leads the hero to feel they can challenge social rules and the gods. Romeo arrogantly believes he can attend Capulet's ball, even though his family is Capulet's greatest enemy. If love had drawn him to the party, we might feel more sympathy for Romeo. But we know it is simple hubris, arrogance which draws him, because we don't believe in Romeo's love. In fact, his reason for going is even worse, he simply wants to win a bet: "I'll go along, no such sight to be shown, But to rejoice in splendour of mine own." Similarly, Juliet believes that she can challenge the social rules of marrying for love, without her parents' consent. The Friar believes he can also marry them without parental consent for the greater good of ending the feud. Tybalt and Mercutio both believe than can survive duels of honour. And so on - hubris, hubris, hubris. In a Greek tragedy, this quality is displayed by the hero. Shakespeare gives it to almost every character, except Benvolio.

4. Hamartia

The hero must have a tragic flaw, which changes his noble character. This tragic flaw is called hamartia. It also includes deeds which are unworthy of a noble hero. We might decide that Romeo's hamartia begins with trying to bribe Rosaline for sex, but certainly happens when he decides to marry Juliet in secret. Juliet's hamartia would also be that secret marriage. However, it's probably true that all the characters suffer from the same hamartia, which is their excessive pride: hubris.

5. Peripeteia

This is a sudden reversal of fortune which happens to the tragic hero or, in Romeo and Juliet, heroes.

We might argue that this is the main plot feature of the whole play, with every character suffering this reversal. Mercutio's death is a reversal of fortune - all the other fights have never led to a killing. Paris's death only happens because Juliet has pretended to be dead. The Friar only helped her do this to stop her committing suicide. Juliet only kills herself because the Friar isn't there to stop her. Juliet only pretends to be dead because her father has found (for Elizabethan times) the perfect husband in Paris. The Prince loses two relatives - Tybalt and Mercutio - because he was too lenient with earlier fights before the play begins. And so on - every solution leads to a worse complication and tragedy.

Romeo's peripeteia is a little different. He sets out to murder Tybalt in proof of his manhood. Once he has succeeded, he treats this as a sudden reversal for himself, rather than for Tybalt. He doesn't blame himself for this, instead he blames 'fortune': **"Oh, I am fortune's fool!"** The audience might simply blame him for his own foolishness.

The letter sent by the Friar warning Romeo of Juliet's feigned death doesn't reach him because there has been an outbreak of plague, a peripeteia for all of Verona.

Romeo's ability to buy poison is an ironic peripeteia, as Romeo tells the apothecary "I pay thy poverty", to give him sudden riches. It is a fantastic reversal of fortune for the apothecary, but death for Romeo.

Juliet's peripeteias are her father's decision to bring forward the wedding to Paris, her joy at surviving the Friar's poison, only to find Romeo already dead, and the Friar leaving her to commit suicide.

The death of the lovers is the peripeteia of both feuding families. Romeo's mother dies because Romeo was exiled. The Prince tells both families, "let mischance be slave to patience", demanding that they turn the peripeteia into a positive lesson. The fathers make peace and each promises to build a golden statue of the other's child.

6. Nemesis

An opponent or rival who can't be beaten. In the modern sense, we use it to mean an arch enemy, and the idea that this enemy cannot be overcome is often lost. But in Shakespeare's time, and in tragedies, a nemesis couldn't be defeated.

In Greek mythology, Nemesis was the name of a goddess, who punished anyone showing hubris against the gods. If we think of Fate as Romeo's nemesis, then Shakespeare suggests his hubris occurred when he defied Fate and attended Capulet's ball.

7. Fate

In Shakespeare's tragedies, characters tend to rush towards their fate, even when they know it in advance. Macbeth knows he is going to become king. But he rushes towards it by killing King Duncan. So, Shakespeare's tragic heroes aren't usually victims of Fate. They are never powerless to stop fate. All they have to do is make a sensible decision to avoid Fate. Instead, they choose to challenge Fate. This is hubris. They challenge Fate, and this leads to their tragic downfall and death.

In Romeo and Juliet, we know the lovers are "star-crossed". Romeo is warned of this by his dream before the Capulet ball which told him of **"some consequence yet hanging in the stars".** So we know that his original hubris was in not listening to Fate's warning. If he hadn't attended the Capulet ball, this fate could have been avoided.

The opposite happens in Greek tragedy. There, the hero tries to avoid their fate - but the very things they try to avoid it end up, ironically, bringing that fate about.

Example

Oedipus was born to king Laius, the king of Thebes. Laius had been told his fate was that his son would kill him. So, he ordered baby Oedipus to be abandoned to die, tied by his foot to a stake, exposed on a mountainside. However, the baby was rescued by a shepherd, who gave the boy to King Polybus of Corinth. Oedipus grew up believing that Polybus was his father.

As a teenager, he asked about his fate from the Oracle at Delphi, and she told him he was destined to kill his father. There were Oracles all over Greece, who told people the future, but the Oracle at Delphi was the most famous. Horrified, and desperate not to kill his father, Oedipus left Corinth and travelled to Thebes. On the road to Thebes, he got into a quarrel with an arrogant man in a chariot. The quarrel turned into a fight, and Oedipus killed the man.

This is the beginning of his tragedy, as the man was King Laius, his own father. He then entered Thebes and after a while married Jocasta, the widowed queen, not knowing that she was his own mother. At this stage, he didn't even know that the man he killed was Laius, the king.

There's much more to the plot, but you can see the main point of the tragedy. The hero tries desperately to avoid their fate, and everything they try brings that fate closer. That's how Greek tragedies work.

8. The World View of Tragedy

We can argue that this way of looking at the world makes sense in the world of the ancient Greeks, with their many Gods interfering in human lives. You were born to a certain status in life, that didn't change, and random disease, violence, invasion, famine etc could claim you and your family at any time.

Shakespeare's England was different. In medieval times (roughly from 500 AD to 1500 AD) a person's status and role in society was decided at birth. The only real way to change that was through promotion in the church or the army. But by Shakespeare's day trade and London had expanded considerably. This created a much greater range of opportunities and new jobs and roles, such as the theatre. Shakespeare was a completely self-made man, among a small group of pioneers who invented modern theatres and plays.

To Elizabethan Londoners the idea that success and failure was not based on your family of birth, or your fate was very attractive. The idea that the individual made real choices and could shape their future was very attractive. Even now, we all like to believe that we are free to choose our own future.

9. The Greek Furies (Erinyes)

These goddesses punished those who had broken social rules and appear in many Greek tragedies. Romeo appears to be praying to them when he asks "fire-eyed fury" to conduct, to lead him. Again, this is hubristic, because he is trying to claim that his desire for revenge is not personal, but something that God would want. Considering that the Christian God is quite specific on this point, "Thou shalt not kill", the audience can see that Romeo is foolish in trying to justify his revenge and proof of manhood.

10. Catharsis

Through tragedy, the audience experience a sense of catharsis. Catharsis means the audience get rid, or purge themselves, of negative emotions such as pity or fear. We can see that Shakespeare has made us feel pity for the lovers' social predicament, and for the extreme passion of their emotions. We pity the parents who have been deceived, especially the Montagues. And Shakespeare has drawn on an undercurrent of fear of invasion, of Catholic revolution or civil war, of the untrustworthiness of servants and our own children. All these are resolved as the lovers meet their deaths, the Friar and the Nurse are exposed, and the social order is restored as Capulet and Montague end the feud.

Top Twenty Reversals of Fortune – Peripeteia

A key feature of tragedy is **Peripeteia** – the reversal of fortune. Shakespeare plays with this idea by flooding the whole play with reversals of fortune. Each one of these is a key turning point – if they didn't happen, one or both of the lovers would not have died.

The Peripeteia is a shift from good luck to bad luck. Because Shakespeare loves to play with his audience, he specialises in bad luck which pretends to be good luck. Disguised Peripeteia! Those are in bold.

1. if only there were no feud

2. if only Rosaline had opened her lap to saint seducing gold

3. **if only the servant with the invitations could read**

4. if only Romeo had listened to his dream

5. if only Lady Capulet hadn't asked Juliet to think about an arranged marriage to Paris

6. If only the Capulets had told Juliet that Paris was going to have to wait for two years to marry her

7. **if only Capulet had Romeo thrown out of the ball when Tybalt asked him**

8. **if only Romeo had not seen Juliet**

9. **if only Romeo had not climbed the garden walls**

10. **if only Juliet hadn't been expressing her thoughts about Romeo out loud from the balcony**

11. **if only Juliet didn't want to get married**

12. if only Romeo wasn't looking to have sex with a Capulet

13. **if only the Friar refused to marry them**

14. if only Romeo hadn't tried to stop Mercutio and Tybalt fighting

15. if only Romeo hadn't killed Tybalt

16. if only there had been no plague

17. if only Balthasar had not told Romeo that Juliet was dead

18. if only both lovers weren't in love with the idea of death

19. if only Romeo had waited a little longer, so Juliet woke up

20. if only the Friar had not left Juliet alone with Romeo's body and dagger

Top Ten Facts About Sonnets

1. A sonnet has 14 lines, each of 10 syllables of iambic pentameter.

2. The rhyme scheme of a Shakespearean sonnet is: abab cdcd efef gg.

3. As you can see, the first 8 lines (called the octave) are divided into 2 quatrains (groups of 4 lines).

4. The Volta in a Petrarchan sonnet occurs after the octave. In Shakespeare's sonnets, the Volta occurs with the final couplet.

5. The Petrarchan sonnet has far fewer choices of rhyme because Italian has so many words ending with similar sounds. His sonnets were divided into two stanzas: an eight-line stanza (octave) rhyming ABBAABBA, and a six-line stanza (sestet) rhyming CDCDCD or CDECDE. Petrarchan sonnets were mainly written to the woman his persona love - Laura - but she did not return that love. He created the unrequited lover. This is why Romeo is attracted to a Capulet, Rosaline, who won't return his love.

6. Romeo begins with the first quatrain of a sonnet. Taking his lead (exactly like a dance), Juliet replies with a quatrain of her own, perfectly continuing the rhyme scheme of his sonnet. This immediately signals to the audience that, though the love is at first sight, it is real. They are suited to each other - completing each other's lines.

7. The genius of this sonnet is that Romeo has planned his seduction with a Petrarchan Volta at line 9. But the sudden twist at line 11 has been better planned by Juliet. 1.

8. Romeo's Volta comes after the octave, just like a Petrarchan sonnet. He seizes his chance to suggest they kiss: "O, then, dear saint, let lips do what hands do." Modesty forbids Juliet from taking the initiative here by kissing him, but we can see that she has led the conversation to make it easier for him to kiss her.

9. Juliet introduces the final Volta as a Shakespearean couplet - Romeo began just trying to kiss her hand, and she has engineered the conversation to make sure that she kisses his lips: "Saints do not move, though grant for prayers' sake."

10. Remember this is the second sonnet of the play, with the first being the prologue which laid out the tragedy. We associate the sonnet with tragedy, as well as love. By having the lovers share the lines of a sonnet as they share their first kiss, Shakespeare is also suggesting this is the moment which seals their tragic fate. This would suggest they are punished for their blasphemous use of religious imagery. We will be reminded of that in the next scene when Juliet calls Romeo "god of her idolatry". This is a direct challenge to god, a classic example of hubris.

Top Ten Interesting Questions Asked on Google

1. Why does Romeo and Juliet start with a fight?

It doesn't though! It starts with the patriarchal wordplay, full of sexual puns, showing contempt for women as sex objects. The fight follows this to show that this violence is produced by the immaturity of young men. Shakespeare wants to link this violence between the families to the exploitation of women. This suggests that Juliet's violent rejection of life and her parents is a response to the way society treats women. It isn't a response to the feud itself.

2. Why does Romeo use oxymorons?

It is easy to see Romeo's oxymorons as a wonderfully inventive example of poetry. However, he uses these to describe his immature love for Rosaline. Instead, Shakespeare wants us to see the oxymorons as a kind of amateur poetry, which Romeo uses desperately, as an attempt to show off. What does "O heavy lightness" mean? Nothing, there has been no lightness, there has been a brawl. Romeo's poetry when he falls in love with Juliet is much more mature. However, as Mercutio points out, it is still not convincing – remember the rhyme of "dove" and "love".

3. Why does Romeo compare Juliet to the sun?

Well, you remember how Shakespeare made fun of this kind of comparison in his own poetry. It also reminds us that Romeo is Phaeton, who spills the sun from his chariot when he crashes it. It suggests that Romeo is both out of control and dangerous to Juliet, as she is the metaphorical "sun" he is going to spill. He does this by committing suicide before Juliet wakes, causing her to choose to die with him.

4. Why does Juliet call Romeo a pilgrim?

It's sacrilegious, continuing Romeo's idea of her as a "shrine". It shows the lovers' hubris. But she is also being incredibly clever, trying to move Romeo away from wanting to kiss the "palm" and kiss the "palmer". It makes her the leader in this meeting, which she continues by telling him to arrange the marriage. She speeds up the relationship so it has a compressed, tragic arc.

5. Why does Capulet arrange a party?

Even Capulet thinks that it has been "Some five and twenty years; and then we mask'd." His cousin thinks it has been longer. So a masked ball is a huge event. Capulet has organised this to impress Paris who, as a rich Count, related to the Prince, is going to expect a very large dowry. This is Capulet's way of showing off the financial strength of his family, as well as the beauty of his daughter Juliet. Although he tells Paris to wait "two more summers" and to look at all the other beautiful single women, "And like her most whose merit most shall be" this might be a negotiating tactic. The extravagant party tells Paris that Capulet does not need Paris' wealth. His invitation to look at other women then suggests that Capulet can find even more wealthy suitors than Paris over the next two years. These cunning tactics make Paris even more desperate and, ironically, bring Juliet's tragic death closer.

6. Why does Mercutio curse both houses and with a plague?

Just like Romeo refused to take responsibility for his decisions when he claims "O, I am fortune's fool!", so Mercutio refuses to take responsibility, blaming "both houses". Shakespeare does this to show that the tragedy is caused by young male immaturity, as he is criticising the patriarchal nature of his society, and the celebration of male honour. Mercutio picks a "plague", rather than simply a "curse" because Shakespeare wants to link it to the actual plague which prevents Romeo getting the Friar's letter. This is Shakespeare's way of also blaming Mercutio for the death of the lovers, as his curse comes true. It is also true that Mercutio has a point – Romeo is also responsible for his death, as Mercutio was killed as a result of Romeo leaving him defenceless. Romeo is able to kill Tybalt very quickly, which implies that Mercutio was right about Tybalt's duelling skill being all show.

7. Why does Mercutio speak in prose?

Remember that prose tells us the speaker is a character of inferior status. This helps us see Mercutio's pursuit of a duel with Tybalt as dishonourable. It emphasises how he is losing control of himself. He is so desperate to see a duel that he jumps in when Romeo refuses. It shows that the duel has not really been a matter of honour for Mercutio, he just wants to prove that Tybalt is merely the "butcher of a silk button", to prove himself superior.

8. Why does Mercutio talk about Queen Mab?

Shakespeare wants to show off Mercutio's quick wits, and his brilliance with imagery. But it also highlights his cynical perspective about love as simply a way of disguising the desire for sex. Similarly, the speech shows that all our desires are corrupt, so he makes Queen Mab visit all sectors of society – the law, the church, the king's court, the army – to show that they are all corrupt. Finally, he builds to the worst aspect of Queen Mab, which is teaching women to suffer the burden of childbirth: **"That presses them, and learns them first to bear"**.

9. Why does Tybalt call Romeo a villain?

Tybalt is obsessed with male status and honour. This is a class-based status. Remember how he looks down on servants as subhuman, "heartless hinds". So "villain" is a powerful insult in Tybalt's eyes, because it strips away that status as a gentleman. It also implies that Romeo is lacking in manners. This is the ultimate insult to Tybalt, because, as Mercutio tells us, he is obsessed with manners and etiquette. He mocks Tybalt as "a gentleman of the very first house" and "the courageous captain of compliments". Tybalt sees his mastery of polite manners as proof of his worth as a "gentleman", whereas Mercutio places no value on manners at all. His insult, "villain", is also therefore comic for the audience. Tybalt's good manners prevent him from using stronger words. It's why he can only hint that Romeo and Mercutio "consort", rather than accuse them directly of being lovers.

10. Why does Tybalt speak in rhyming couplets?

Rhyming couplets are used for these reasons. To indicate:

- A character has a noble status – by birth, and sometimes also through their personal characteristics.
- A character has wisdom, or has thought through their words carefully in advance.
- A character's depth of feeling and passion.
- An ending to a scene, powerful moment in a character's life, or their actual end or death.

Tybalt's couplets reflect all of these except 'wisdom' and 'noble personal characteristics'.

Part 5: How to Write an Essay

When you read the section on each character, your best revision is to turn each section into a 700-1000 word essay. Choose the word total you can reproduce in a 45 minute exam.

Top Ten Exam Questions

These are the questions asked by the main exam boards when they first introduced the literature exams. I've organised them into the Top Ten Topics.

Because they are the first questions asked, we can infer that the examiners also considered them the most important questions to be asked. This means they are highly likely to recur each year.

How does Shakespeare present:

1. Lord Capulet / Lord Capulet and Juliet

2. Love

3. Romeo

4. Juliet

5. Mercutio

6. Male behaviour / Family honour in the play

7. Tybalt / The relationship between Mercutio and Tybalt

8. The Friar

9. The relationships between older and younger characters

10. Power

Top Ten Words to Use in an Essay

1. Patriarchal
2. Masculinity
3. Hubris
4. Metaphor
5. Allusion
6. Undermines
7. Tragedy
8. Ironic
9. Sexual

10. Romantic

Note: you can change the endings of each word.

Example

Let's use the ten words to answer part of question 1 above.

Shakespeare uses the unequal power relationship between Capulet and his daughter Juliet to explore the evils of **patriarchal** society. He wants to show that male power is damaging to women, especially in the form of sexual exploitation. Initially, he wants to delay the marriage to Paris, as he believes becoming a young bride and mother may have "too early marr'd" his own wife. He consequently wishes Paris to wait until she is sixteen and "ripe" for marriage. However, this **metaphor** reveals the corruption of his **masculine** view. Even though he claims to be protecting his daughter, this ripeness likens her to a crop, to be grown and harvested. This perfectly describes society's view of women, owned by their fathers until they are sold.

This language is both sensual and **sexual**. He extends this when Juliet refuses to marry Paris, instructing her to "fettle your fine joints". This fricative alliteration echoes the common word for intercourse, and he leaves Juliet in little doubt that her "fine joints" should be used to sexually satisfy her husband. Choosing the verb "fettle" isn't just for alliterative effect, but also portrays her body as a piece of pottery, to be moulded. This forces Juliet to see her worth only as an object, and as a sexual object which can be shaped and moulded to fit the desires of others – of a father and a husband. Capulet's **hubris** is that he believes he can control his daughter through threats, taunting her as "carrion", literally disposable meat, and as "baggage" which he can throw out on "the streets" or give to Paris, his "friend". However, his cruelty **undermines** his control. By withdrawing empathy and financial support he makes Juliet much more likely to choose suicide as a way to avoid a bigamous marriage with Paris.

Juliet's **tragedy** is brought about by the speed of her marriage to Romeo. The conventional interpretation is that Juliet is motivated by love, comparing him to "a rose" and declaring her love for him in soliloquy. However, her focus on "any other part belonging to a man" **undermines** this view of **romantic** love, and suggests she is at least in part motivated by sexual desire. She cannot simply act on this because patriarchal society insists she remain a virgin until marriage. She manoeuvres Romeo into proposing, insisting that if his "purpose [is] marriage" he has to organise this by the next day. She reminds him of what a catch she is in patriarchal terms, telling him that she will give him "all my fortunes". This **alludes** to the wealth he will achieve through her dowry, which the Nurse reminds him of with "the chinks" and which he takes to heart, telling the Friar that he is going to marry the daughter of "rich Capulet".

The **irony** of this is that Capulet's suggestion that she should meet Paris as a prospective husband accelerates Juliet's desire to escape this fate. Yet her only way to escape is to trap herself in another marriage, with a lover of her own choosing. Capulet therefore creates the circumstances which will lead to Juliet's death.

Shakespeare also asks us to consider how much Juliet is also motivated by rebelling against her father. When she asks "what's in a name" she appears to be lamenting that Romeo is a Montague.

But an alternative is that this makes Romeo an even more exciting husband, because he is exactly the wrong choice for her father. Shakespeare invites us to wonder about this as he presents Romeo as attracted to rebelling against the feud in the same way. Romeo believes himself in love with a Capulet, Rosaline, and falls instantly in love at the ball which is full of Capulet women.

By framing their romantic love in this way, Shakespeare asks us to examine the role of Capulet in the tragedy, both as a promoter of the feud and abuser of his patriarchal power in forcing Juliet into an early marriage. In doing this, Capulet and his daughter represent the injustice of forced marriages in Elizabethan society.

(Notice that this approach means that this answer to question 1 could easily be made to fit questions 2, 9 and even 10).

Top Ten Implications for Your Revision

1. We can see that the examiners go out of their way to avoid asking you about Romeo and Juliet on their own – the Friar is just as likely to come up as a character on his own.

2. However, the examiners are really interested in Romeo and Juliet from the perspective of love, so focusing on their attitude to love is essential. When you are writing about love you need to evaluate how much is genuine, how much is rebellion against social and family expectations, and how much is simply sexual desire.

3. The male characters appear to be much more interesting to the examiners than the female characters. So revise male attitudes in the play, and what this says about the patriarchal society. The question on family honour is just another way of writing about the patriarchal society.

4. Lord Capulet is the most popular character to look at, so think about how he controls other characters. This is another question about patriarchal society and the control of women through marriage, sex and reproduction.

5. The most popular theme is about power in the play. This is just another way of reframing your revision about the patriarchal society. Here you will look at the effect of male power on male and female characters.

6. The questions about Mercutio and Tybalt are really questions about sex and power and male relationships. So, this is really a question about the patriarchal society, concentrating on these two characters. You will notice that they have a lot to do with Romeo too.

7. Revise Tybalt and Mercutio together. The examiners seem scared of asking you about Mercutio and Romeo together because that just unlocks a door into a room full of sexual content they can't expect your teachers to have taught you. If you get a question just on Tybalt, you can use the essay you revised above on Tybalt's relationship with Mercutio and Romeo. If you get a question just on Mercutio, you can use the essay you revised above on Mercutio's relationship with Tybalt and Romeo.

8. If you get a question on the Nurse or Lady Capulet, it will always be answered by writing about their relationship with Juliet.

9. None of the questions ask you directly about tragedy and fate. This must mean that the examiners think this is a concept only top-grade students will understand. Therefore, revising how far fate is responsible for the tragedy will help you add this theme into any essay. However, they can ask you about fate in disguise. If you get a question about the Friar, this is really a question about fate. Revise how important the Friar's decisions are in causing the deaths of the lovers.

10. None of the questions ask "why" Shakespeare presents characters in particular ways. This means that examiners believe that understanding Shakespeare's purpose and relevant context is only for top grade candidates. You should prepare this so you can add relevant details to every question.

Top Ten Thesis Statements

1. Shakespeare sets the play in Verona so that he can explore the effects of a violent, patriarchal society on its young people. He uses the tragedy of Romeo and Juliet and the deaths of Mercutio, Tybalt and Paris to illustrate the evils of a society based on male honour, and treating women as male property to be exploited.

2. Shakespeare writes the play largely in verse and rhyme in order to treat it as a dramatised love poem. His imagery and plotting charts the extremes of emotion that link love both to hope and despair. He explores the obsessive attraction to the other as the death of identity and self, and shows how the logical ending to the obsessive love is the death of the lover.

3. Shakespeare writes the tragedy as a satire on civilised behaviour. He shows that the conventions around patriarchal marriage have tragic consequences for women. He shows how the etiquette of male honour and duelling lead inevitably to death. Finally, he reveals that love is simply dressed up in poetic emotion and cliché in order to hide what it truly is, sexual lust.

4. Shakespeare writes this tragic tale to help his audience revisit the passions of their youth and empathise with the power of unchecked, uncynical and profound emotion. Through the cathartic tragedy of the lovers' deaths, and their unity in the afterlife, he helps his audience pity their fate, and re-examine the role of love in their own lives.

5. Shakespeare writes the play to tap into social anxiety. He links the loyalty and betrayal of servants to the loyalty and obedience of children. He takes the fear of Catholic invasion or uprising and creates the manipulative Friar Lawrence to Stoke those fears. Finally, he takes the end of reign anxiety about Elizabeth's succession, and recasts fear of civil war as a family feud which kills all their children.

6. Shakespeare creates Capulet to magnify the injustice of patriarchal control of women. He shows the hypocrisy of infidelity and the lack of love towards wives and daughters through arranged marriages.

7. Shakespeare creates Mercutio as a counterpoint to Romeo's obsession with love. He shows that young men are almost always motivated by sexual desire. Shakespeare also uses Mercutio to explore male homosexual love. Finally, Mercutio helps discredit the ideals of male honour and duelling.

8. Shakespeare creates Tybalt to illustrate the dangers of masculine honour and pursuit of status and reputation. He is the antithesis of quick-witted Mercutio, but shares his arrogance, vanity and distrust of women. Shakespeare kills both men for their hubris, and Tybalt's homophobia.

9. Shakespeare creates Friar Lawrence to discredit the Catholic church, but also to illustrate the wisdom and medicinal knowhow which was lost with the dissolution of the monasteries. He uses the Friar's adult perspective to contrast with the lovers' youthful passion and promote the idea of balance.

10. Shakespeare creates the Nurse to dramatise the damage of early marriage, childbirth, child mortality and the sacrifices made by the servant classes. She reveals how patriarchal society ruins women's lives and corrupts their thinking.

Top Ten Romeo Quotes

Selecting only 10 quotations for the main characters is kind of crazy – you have to reject so many great ones to get to your final list. In my selection with Romeo I have tried to rate each quotation by what it tells us about all aspects of his personality and character development. In this way, they would help you answer any essay on Romeo with some interesting perspectives.

1. "Nor ope her lap to saint-seducing gold".

Here we see how Romeo represents the patriarchal society, seeing women as property to be bought. The problem isn't that Rosaline doesn't love Romeo, but that her price is too high. The sibilance also emphasises how sinister this view of women is.

2. "I fear too early: for my mind misgives
Some consequence yet hanging in the stars,
Shall bitterly begin his fearful date
With this night's revels"

In Greek tragedy, the tragic hero tries everything to avoid their fate, but their hamartia means that every choice they make ironically brings their fate closer. In Shakespeare's tragedy, the hamartia is the character's hubris. They refuse to try to escape their fate, and often seem to rush towards it. Romeo's hubris is that he ignores fate's warning, and goes to the ball anyway.

3. "O, she doth teach the torches to burn bright!
It seems she hangs upon the cheek of night
As a rich jewel in an Ethiop's ear;
Beauty too rich for use, for earth too dear!
So shows a snowy dove trooping with crows"

Although Romeo celebrates Juliet's beauty, the imagery is also full of warnings of fate. Her beauty makes the torches burn brighter, because she is so bright. But comparing her to a torch's light also invites us to associate her with a flame which will burn too brightly, and then die.

Juliet is exotic, like a rich Ethiopian in Elizabethan London. But the Ethiopian is also racially different, a symbol of conflict, of not fitting in, a clue that Romeo and Juliet's marriage is not a good match. (Shakespeare returned to this racial conflict in **Othello**).

The idea that her beauty is "for earth too dear" implies that it will only find a home in heaven. This implies her death.

The "dove" is chosen for its symbolism with love, and also its white purity. But "snowy" doesn't just imply whiteness, it is also cold and wintry and suggests death. So too does the symbolism of being surrounded by "crows". Romeo means it to show how ugly all the other dancing women are compared to Juliet. But the symbolism of "crows" depends on their blackness. This of course is a reminder of death. It also makes the "Ethiop's" blackness a link to death as well.

So, the symbolism keeps suggesting that Romeo chooses death for Juliet when he chooses her.

4. "If I profane with my unworthiest hand
This holy shrine, the gentle sin is this,
My lips, two blushing pilgrims, ready stand
To smooth that rough touch with a tender kiss."

The religious imagery attached to Romeo's pursuit of sex is sacrilegious, almost blasphemous. Even if Romeo is not pursuing sex, but simply declaring his love, the imagery is still a challenge to God. However, we can see from the physical nature of his imagery – "hand, lips, blushing, touch, kiss" – that sex is still very much in his thinking.

5. "wilt thou leave me so unsatisfied?"

This is a tricky line because of the staging. The Curtain theatre had a balcony, so Juliet is inaccessible there until Romeo arranges for a ladder once they are married. Baz Luhrmann saw this line as a clear declaration that Romeo wants a sexual encounter with Juliet, so he filmed it with Romeo climbing up to the balcony. Shakespeare gives Romeo this sexual language, but stages the scene so that Romeo cannot physically reach Juliet. Perhaps this helps explain his quick acceptance of Juliet's demand that they should marry – it is the only way he can get up to her balcony and have sex with her.

6. "My nyas?"

Both lovers see themselves as the falconer, and their lover as the falcon. This immediately suggests that they see each other very differently. They are actually in conflict. It is a metaphor which suggests that the marriage is not a good match. But the sport of falconry involves hunting. Here, they actually hunt each other, in that they cause each other's death. There is a patriarchal layer here as well. The nyas is a young hawk, still to be trained. Romeo doesn't just imply that he wants to control Juliet in this metaphor. He also links that to her youth: because she is so young, she will be easier to control. This makes his love less romantic!

7. "Tybalt, the reason that I have to love thee
Doth much excuse the appertaining rage
To such a greeting. Villain am I none;
Therefore farewell; I see thou know'st me not."

Romeo could simply have replied with the words beginning at "Villain". This would be a factual reply that is impossible to misunderstand. A "villain" did not have the modern meaning of criminal – it was an insult about class – a "villain" was a person of low birth status, with no manners or refinement. In the early 21st Century, a modern equivalent might be 'chav'. This insult had more power because Elizabethan society was such a class-based society, and because gentlemen and nobles were expected to display ritualised good manners. However, the tricky part for Romeo is that to refuse to duel is to break with noblemen's etiquette. This is why he feels he must offer the explanation that he now has a secret reason to "love" Tybalt. He goes on to repeat his "love" twice more. To Tybalt, the logical explanation is that Romeo is mocking his sexuality. This arguably causes his rage which encourages him to fight Mercutio, and then also to cheat, stabbing Mercutio when he is undefended. Shakespeare is showing us that Romeo's "love" is the cause of the tragedy – it leads to all the deaths in the play. Even his mother dies because of her love for him.

8. "sweet Juliet,
Thy beauty hath made me effeminate
And in my temper soften'd valour's steel."

Well, so much for love. Who does he blame for Mercutio's death? Juliet. Yes, just as Eve ruined Adam, so Juliet has ruined Romeo, emasculating him. She has caused him to go against his male nature, and adopt an inferior, female "effeminate" nature. He has lost his "valour". Shakespeare links this directly to Romeo's killing of Tybalt, and the cause of the tragedy. Rather than using Juliet as a reason not to kill Tybalt, Romeo now uses her as the reason why he must. So, Shakespeare is deeply critical of this view of masculinity, and of this dismissal of peace and non-violence as a female characteristic. Romeo, you fool, he seems to be saying.

9. "O, I am fortune's fool!"

First, he blames Juliet. Now he blames "fortune", or fate. He claims that his tragedy is inevitable. This is accurate in a Greek tragedy. But not in a Shakespearean one – every decision Romeo has made has seemed like a mistake at the time. It isn't as though he has simply not understood the consequences when he makes each decision – he has weighed up the consequences and done it anyway – going to the ball, kissing Juliet there, climbing Juliet's garden wall, marrying her, and now deciding to kill Tybalt. Yet Romeo refuses to face the facts, that his "fate" is largely written by his own hand. He is a "fool", but can we blame "fortune"?

10. "O, give me thy hand,
One writ with me in sour misfortune's book.
I'll bury thee in a triumphant grave."

Why this quotation instead of the poetry describing his dead Juliet? Because this is the most problematic part of the play – the part which is often cut. Why does Romeo agree to place Paris in the tomb with Juliet? It's because it fits his conscience to believe that none of this has been his fault, that it is the working of "misfortune" or fate. He believes his "hand" and Paris's "hand" have been written in fate's book. To understand this, you have to know the secondary meaning of hand – it is short for handwriting. He means that Paris and he have both been "writ" – their names and fates have been written in "misfortune's book". They are both tragic heroes. This is why, as a hero, Paris deserves a "triumphant grave", like Romeo.

But Shakespeare's imagery also undermines this. The handwriting is their own – both Paris and Romeo have written their own names in "misfortune's book" through their arrogance and hubris. Shakespeare reminds us that this is a tragedy. And tragic heroes are always partly responsible for their fate.

Top Ten Juliet Quotes

1. "It is an honour that I dream not of."

But this is a lie! We soon find out that she has dreamed of marriage - because she instructs Romeo to marry her that same night. If there is anything she disapproves of, it is the "honour" of having a husband chosen for her. We can see that she uses the word "honour" ironically. As we see when she speaks to her mother after Tybalt's death, she is skilled at making her mother believe her words are sincere, though she means the opposite.

2. Juliet's Volta:

> **"JULIET: Saints do not move, though grant for prayers' sake.**
> **ROMEO: Then move not while my prayer's effect I take."**

Although we would expect Romeo to woo Juliet, this being a patriarchal society and all, it comes as something of a surprise to see that she is in charge of the seduction. She manoeuvres Romeo toward kissing her lips instead of her hand. She manoeuvres him into marriage. It's the old Adam and Eve Original Sin all over again, the woman leading the man astray. That's one interpretation Shakespeare's audience would be ready for.

But I prefer the interpretation that Shakespeare is attacking that patriarchal view of women's greater capacity to sin. What forces her into marriage? Patriarchal society which prizes virginity so highly. What forces her to marry so quickly? The patriarchal rush to get her married to Paris. So, marriage to Romeo is the only logical escape.

3. "What's Montague? It is nor hand nor foot,
Nor arm nor face nor any other part
Belonging to a man. Oh, be some other name!
What's in a name? That which we call a rose
By any other word would smell as sweet."

We use these lines to think about the nature of "fortune": if only Romeo hadn't been a Montague, no tragedy would have happened. But Romeo is addicted to Capulets. First, there was Rosaline. Shakespeare introduced her identity as a Capulet, which wasn't in Brooke's poem. Then Romeo gate crashes the Capulet ball, so that there is a very high chance of meeting many more Capulet women. So "fortune" has had a giant helping hand from Romeo.

Mercutio makes fun of Romeo's love poetry, describing Rosaline's face, when he is really thinking of her "quivering thigh", etc. Because Juliet is speaking to herself, her thoughts follow exactly the same pattern, ending with a coy reference to "any other part Belonging to a man". She too is thinking about sex.

Notice how she changes Romeo into "rose" and how she focuses on his "smell". We can argue that this is just a metaphor, and doesn't specifically describe Romeo. But look at what has just gone before – she is focused entirely on his body, his physicality.

The "rose" is also a feminine metaphor. It prepares us for Romeo's sudden decision to justify killing Tybalt. He tells himself that Juliet has made him "effeminate", and perhaps that starts here, when he hears her first linking him to "a rose".

4. "Hist, Romeo, hist! O for a falconer's voice/ To lure this tassel-gentle back again."

Earlier in this scene, Romeo imagined himself with "light wings." In these lines, Juliet picks up on this image to picture Romeo as a tame falcon and herself as a falconer. Juliet's image suggests she feels she has power over him. The fact that she takes Romeo's metaphor and bends it to her own purposes also suggests her sense of power in their relationship.

But she also realises that this power might not be real, which is why she doesn't have "a falconer's voice". She is calling back her "falcon" without knowing if he will actually return. Notice how she also describes him as a "tassel-gentle". This was the name for a Peregrine falcon. Not only was this the falcon most associated with royalty, she also focuses on its other name because it includes the word "gentle". She believes Romeo is going to be a "gentle" husband. Perhaps this will make him easier for her to control, as the falconer in the metaphor.

5. "Thy purpose marriage, send me word tomorrow
By one that I'll procure to come to thee
Where and what time thou wilt perform the rite,
And all my fortunes at thy foot I'll lay
And follow thee my lord throughout the world."

Here comes the patriarchy and Juliet's forward thinking. She knows that she and Romeo think they are in love, and definitely want to enjoy sex together. She insists on "marriage", because that is the only way society will allow her to enjoy sex. She also knows that Romeo might change his mind, so she insists on arranging the marriage by "tomorrow". She knows that her parents are likely to make an early marriage with Paris, so again, another reason to have a marriage to Romeo arranged by "tomorrow". She also realises that Romeo lives in the same patriarchal world, and would not marry simply for love, because his status means that he will be able to marry wealth as well as beauty. Love, she knows, won't be enough for the son of a lord. So, she reminds him that he will have "all my fortunes". Rather than simply mean 'all my wealth', she includes the other meaning of "fortune" as luck and fate – it is the equivalent of the marriage vow, "for better or worse, in sickness and in health". This makes it more romantic, rather than a purely financial exchange.

We know this has a huge impact on Romeo because he actually arranges the marriage to take place "tomorrow" rather than simply be arranged for a future date. It also prompts him to tell Friar Lawrence that she is the daughter of "*rich* Capulet" – the financial exchange suits him very well. It is also a way of telling the Friar that the marriage is a great patriarchal match, which his parents would definitely support (if only Juliet were not a Capulet).

6. "Come, gentle night, come, loving black-browed night,
Give me my Romeo, and when I shall die,
Take him and cut him out in little stars."

Juliet personifies "night" as a lover. She asks it to "come" twice because she is desperate for Romeo, her actual lover, to arrive. "Night" is a homophone for 'knight', so she gives him black hair, "loving black-browed" knight. "Die" is Elizabethan slang for orgasm. Normally this would be a secondary meaning and "when I shall die" would mean 'when I am dead'. But in context, leaping from her wedding night to her death is a very long leap, a very illogical thought to have. So perhaps the slang meaning is uppermost in her mind. Cutting Romeo "out in little stars" is a desire to turn him into a constellation named after heroes. In this case, Romeo will be her hero because he has caused her to "die". Shakespeare loves this irony – so Juliet will indeed "die" as a result of consummating the marriage with Romeo.

7. "I'll to my wedding bed. And death, not Romeo, take my maidenhead!"

Juliet appears to tell the Nurse that, now Romeo is banished, she will commit suicide. But even now, her last words are about sex. She desperately wants to share her virginity, her "maidenhead" with Romeo. Shakespeare keeps contrasting the depth of her love with the extremes of her sexual desire. This prompts the Nurse to fetch Romeo, and keep Juliet alive, which suggests that she thinks Juliet's threat is real.

Both the last two quotations have linked sex with violence and death. Perhaps Shakespeare is pointing out that the patriarchal rules forbidding sex before marriage are dangerous, leading lovers to extremes which result in violence and death.

8. '"Romeo is banishèd." To speak that word,
Is father, mother, Tybalt, Romeo, Juliet,
All slain, all dead. "Romeo is banishèd."
There is no end, no limit, measure, bound,
In that word's death.'

Brooke's poem portrayed the lovers as sinful, betraying their families and deserving their punishment of tragic death. Shakespeare allows his audience to make their own decisions, and never instructs us how to feel.

Here Juliet thinks of Romeo being "banished" as causing more grief than Tybalt and her parents being killed. She realises this seems like a callous disregard for her parents, and so adds her own death to the mix. But that doesn't convince, because she would not be able to grieve being dead herself. She would rather that her parents were killed in exchange for Romeo being in Verona rather than banished to Mantua.

This certainly sounds like a betrayal, and a warning to parents that they can never trust their teenage children. It also makes Juliet's love just as obsessive as Romeo's. He also tells the Friar that banishment is worse than death. The Friar is able to convince Romeo that he is wrong, but he isn't able to convince Juliet.

We could argue that this is simply because she is so much younger and immature. This would paint the marriage as a rebellion against parental control. Or we could argue that in the patriarchal society, she simply has much more to lose than a man. If Romeo is banished, she could be forced to marry Paris (or whichever suitor her father settles on). She will be "sold". Now she is rebelling against the whole social structure which simply treats daughters as possessions to be traded for power and wealth.

9. "Good father, I beseech you on my knees, Hear me with patience but to speak a word."

Baz Luhrmann portrayed Lord Capulet as drunk in this scene. He noted the sudden change in marriage plans to Paris, from waiting two years to waiting only two days, and decided he needed an extreme reason for Capulet's extreme change of mind.

Shakespeare is much more interested in the patriarchal reasons for the change of mind. He changed this from Brooke's poem, where the marriage is actually Juliet's mother's idea. He is interested in the male agenda: Juliet is property which Capulet wants to give to his "friend".

Juliet knows that she is powerless in this male world. She has to call her father "good", even while he is threatening to send her out into the streets to become a beggar or a prostitute. She literally gets to her "knees" as she would pray in church. She is dramatising how male power is similar to the power of God in how much control it has over a woman's life.

She asks for as little as possible, "but to speak a word", but he doesn't even give her a single word, while he rants at her, insults her, and threatens her for numerous lines. By denying Juliet a voice, Shakespeare shows how all daughters are denied a voice. She says "Hear me" and the iambic pentameter puts the emphasis on "me". It is a plea for identity, and for her own identity to be seen by her father.

Shakespeare's point is not that Juliet is unlucky in having this particular, unreasonable father. His point is that all father daughter relationships in the wealthy classes are just as unlucky for the powerless daughter.

10. "O happy dagger. This is thy sheath."

Juliet unites so many themes here. Juliet's final words link violence, death and sexuality together again. The dagger is a metaphor for the phallus, and the sheath, her body, is also a metaphor for the vagina. In this metaphor, Romeo's dagger enters her one last time. This is one reason she imagines it as "happy", because they are going to be united again in death. Although it is a romantic image, it is also deeply unsettling. Shakespeare also leaves us with the idea that sexual desire has killed the lovers.

The refusal of each to live without the other is also romantic on the surface. But it also hints at the other theme, how in love they each are with the idea of death. If Romeo hadn't associated love with death, he would have remained alive by Juliet's side to witness her miraculous resurrection. We are reminded of Juliet's first reaction to the Nurse, when she thought Romeo had died – she immediately assumed he had taken his own life, **"Hath Romeo slain himself?"** Similarly, if Juliet weren't in love with the idea of death, she might also survive.

If we think back over all the imagery each lover has used to describe the other and themselves, we remember that are mismatched – their strange use of sun and moon imagery, the effeminate use of a rose to describe Romeo, the way each imagines themselves as the falconer and so on. But in their love of death, they are perfectly in unison.

Top Ten Nurse Quotes

1. "Now, by my maidenhead at twelve year old, / I bade [Juliet] come"

Remember that Juliet's marriage at 13 was not a commonplace Elizabethan tradition. The average age of marriage was similar in Elizabethan society as it was for the whole of the 20th century, mid-twenties. In noble families, parents might arrange younger marriages to secure desirable family alliances, but even then, the tradition was not for them to have early sex and risk childbirth – the bride would live with the groom's mother until she was old enough.

This tradition of young marriage is presented as Italian and foreign. The Nurse, who has a very low social status, also married incredibly young, at "twelve". This is a shocking revelation, even to an Elizabethan.

So how does Shakespeare make this history of young marriage relevant to an English audience? He uses it to suggest the dangers of patriarchal control. If society treats women as property, young marriage is a logical outcome. Young girls are easier to control than grown women. Being young, they can produce more children, and provide a better chance of providing a living male heir. By taking patriarchal control to this extreme, Shakespeare is asking his audience to look at the consequences of patriarchal control.

By giving these words to the Nurse, he is also asking women in the audience to question their beliefs. The Nurse seems proud to have lost her virginity so young – it is a badge of honour. It reveals her impatience for Juliet to marry and enjoy sex, which also explains her willingness to help her marry Romeo. In other words, the Nurse has internalised patriarchal control and instead of seeing it as oppressive, sees it as both natural and desirable. In this way Shakespeare asks the women of his audience to look at their own lives and see how much control of their own lives they have accepted as normal. The key autobiographical evidence to support Shakespeare's questioning of patriarchal control of women is his finances. Imagine living in London for twenty years and becoming both successful and rich. Now imagine sending that wealth home to Stratford, buying your family a luxurious home while you buy yourself … nothing. You pay to live in lodgings, you rent a few rooms in someone else's house. This is not someone who believed that men's interests were much more important than women's.

2. "Come Lammas Eve at night shall she be fourteen. Susan and she, God rest all Christian souls Were of an age."

Shakespeare wants us to sympathise with the Nurse, so he gives us a lot of her back story. First, he told us she was married at twelve. Now we find out she had a daughter, Susan, who has died. Then we find out that this daughter was a similar age to Juliet, which means we can easily see how deep a bond she has made with Juliet, how she feels like a mother to her. The Friar tells us later that the Nurse still sleeps in Juliet's bedroom, and we infer that her relationship with Juliet is much stronger than Juliet's with Lady Capulet.

But, as always, there is a level of irony and tragedy. The Nurse is a wet-nurse, which means that she has had to share half her milk with Juliet. It is entirely possible that Susan died within her first three years because Juliet would get the greater portion. Being a wet-nurse to Juliet might well have helped cause Susan's death.

Whether we make that connection or not, Shakespeare also uses the fact of Susan's death thematically. The Nurse points out the similarities between Susan and Juliet, who were "of an age". The other similarity we know from the Prologue, is that Juliet will also be dead.

In this play, men are killed by violence. The women, perhaps Susan, Romeo's mother and Juliet are killed by love. (We can argue that Romeo is also killed by love, and through taking poison, also dies like a woman). We probably feel more sympathy for the women's deaths, or those not caused by violence.

3. "'Yea,' quoth he, 'dost thou fall upon thy face?
Thou wilt fall backward when thou hast more wit;
Wilt thou not, Jule?'"

In Brooke's poem, the Nurse is a terrible gossip, who gets banished at the end. Shakespeare wants to explore her more as a real person. Although he still uses all the servants for comedy, Shakespeare also uses them to explore social issues. Here, the social issue is patriarchal control of women for breeding heirs.

The Nurse's husband laughs at Juliet as a three-year-old, and begins talking to her about her role to have sex. He actually presents sex as a cure for the pain of falling on her "face", as falling on her back will be more pleasurable. The Nurse still finds this hilarious because she loves all mention of sex, and particularly looks forward to Juliet losing her virginity.

Juliet's reaction is interesting. She says "Ay", agreeing that when she has "more wit" she will "fall backward". We know Shakespeare loves irony. As a three-year-old, she did not know what the Nurse's husband meant. But now, she will use her "wit" to marry Romeo, and then will "fall backward" to consummate the wedding. We get the idea that the urge to marry young has been cultivated since she was a toddler. Shakespeare wants us to be critical of this upbringing and society.

4. "I tell you, he that can lay hold of her / Shall have the chinks."

It's very easy to see Romeo and Juliet as a simple love story with a tragic fate. Shakespeare wants more than that. Love, he implies, is never just love in a patriarchal society. The Nurse voices the social opinion that the most important part of courtship is financial. She portrays Juliet as property that a suitor "can lay hold of", and then points out the value of that property, as being worth "the chinks".

This means that the Nurse has bought into the patriarchal way of thinking that she actually celebrates the idea of Juliet as high value property. What might Shakespeare want us to make of this? Perhaps to conclude that the root of the tragedy is not the feud, but Capulet's entitlement to choose a husband for his daughter. If he did not have that right, there would be no need for the Friar's potion, and neither of the lovers would kill themselves.

5. "But first let me tell ye, if ye should lead her in a fool's paradise, as they say, it were a very gross kind of behaviour, as they say; for the gentlewoman is young."

Shakespeare makes sure that the Nurse doesn't question her own beliefs. He wants us to do this though. She is happy to start Juliet thinking about sex from the age of three. She is happy to tell a complete stranger that Juliet is worth a fortune to whoever can "lay hold of her". Now she warns Romeo to treat Juliet with honesty because Juliet "is young". This should alarm her – it clearly suggests that she is also too young for marriage. She also knows that the Capulets want a wedding with Paris, so her secret marriage to Romeo is "a fool's paradise" that the Nurse herself is leading Juliet to. Without the Nurse as an accomplice, Juliet cannot marry Romeo. But she never seems to question the wisdom of helping Juliet in this way, or the consequences when both sets of parents find out.

6. "NURSE: I am the drudge, and toil in your delight;
But you shall bear the burden soon at night.
Go. I'll to dinner; hie you to the cell.

JULIET: Hie to high fortune! Honest Nurse, farewell."

When the Nurse betrays the Capulets and arranges Juliet's marriage, Shakespeare does something surprising. He makes her speak in iambic pentameter, rather than her normal prose. If he wanted to emphasise the betrayal, and therefore her low status, prose would be the conventional fit. But instead, he gives her the language of the nobility. She even speaks in a rhyming couplet.

Juliet makes a rhyming couplet to finish the scene, using the Nurse's rhyme. Shakespeare uses this to emphasise that they are united at this moment. The switch from prose also suggests that he gives it the status of a noble act. Perhaps the marriage is not reckless and a "fool's paradise" after all. Like the Friar, the Nurse could be helping the marriage for noble reasons. Remember, the Prologue suggests that the marriage has to take place, because only the lovers' deaths can stop the feud: **"And the continuance of their parents' rage, Which, but their children's end, nought could remove"**. This implies that the marriage is part of Fate's, and therefore God's, plan.

However, the Nurse's words are also a warning. Although Juliet will have the "delight" of the wedding and the consummation, sex is also painful and dangerous, so Juliet **"shall bear the burden soon at night"**. Sex suddenly doesn't seem as exciting in reality as it does in imagination. The "burden" can be immediate, in that it is initially painful, especially for a thirteen-year-old. But it will also definitely be a "burden" when she gets pregnant and has to give birth.

Shakespeare uses the Nurse to echo Mercutio's anger at how sexual desire is exploited to ruin the lives of women: **"This is the hag, when maids lie on their backs, That presses them, and learns them first to bear"**. He uses his minor characters to warn of the terrible consequences of young motherhood.

7. "Stand up, stand up; stand, and you be a man.
For Juliet's sake, for her sake, rise and stand.
Why should you fall into so deep an O?"

Once again, Shakespeare gives the nurse iambic pentameter, which is a sign that we should pay close attention to what she says. Here she criticises Romeo's youth and immature response to his banishment, where he literally falls on the floor sobbing like a toddler. She reminds him of his duty to "be a man" because he now has responsibilities as a husband. His weeping reaction is so ridiculous that she appears to make up a name for it, as "so deep an O". We can argue that the Nurse's point of view is given status by being in pentameter, and Shakespeare wants his audience to agree with her.

Shakespeare also gives her this language because it is also very sexual. We get the impression that the Nurse is oblivious to the innuendo. The "O" is the O-thing, as Mercutio taught us, representing the vagina. "Why" is a question here, but in Elizabethan English it also had the meaning of 'because'. So the sentence can be read as an instruction to fall deep into that O – an instruction to have sex. This is coupled with the three repetitions of "stand" which is slang for an erection. This pun actually started the play with Sampson and Gregory, "Me they shall feel while I am able to stand: and 'tis known I am a pretty piece of flesh."

So, what is Shakespeare up to? He is suggesting that the main cause of the tragedy is sexual desire. Just as with the opening, he achieves that through comedy: the audience is aware that the nurse is speaking in sexual terms, while she is completely unaware.

8. "Go girl; seek happy nights to happy days".

The alliteration of "Go girl" conveys the Nurse's excitement that Juliet is going to have sex with Romeo. She sees this as completely natural and welcome, as we see with the repetition of "happy". She sees the wedding as a moral choice; she has helped arrange it because she knows Juliet will be "happy" with Romeo rather than with Paris. Shakespeare has made her tell us that she herself was married at twelve so that we can see the Nurse really does want the best for Juliet.

But he also expects his audience to feel uncomfortable about this. Juliet is still a "girl". How many "happy nights" can she have before she gets pregnant? This is why he will later get the Nurse to describe the nights as a "burden".

9. "NURSE: God in heaven bless her.
You are to blame, my lord, to rate her so...I speak no treason...

CAPULET: Peace, you mumbling fool!"

Remember that the Brooke poem portrayed the lovers, the Friar and the Nurse as traitors, betraying the parents and their duties towards them. Shakespeare casts the Nurse in a different light. He suggests that the Nurse might not be a traitor: "I speak no treason". Here, she is resolutely on Juliet's side, telling Capulet he is "to blame". Although Shakespeare might expect his audience to blame both her and the lovers, he also wants us to sympathise with them, to root for them even though we know the lovers will die.

How does she think Capulet is to blame? Here "rate" means 'berate', to verbally attack, so she is blaming him for the temper of his words and threats. But "rate" also has a different meaning, to assess or judge worth. So, in this reading she is also accusing Capulet of measuring Juliet's worth to him as a possession he can exchange for a marriage alliance with Paris. In this reading, the tragedy is not caused by the lovers, but by patriarchal society, where men control women in such damaging ways.

As if to emphasise this control, she is simply dismissed as a "mumbling fool".

We can, of course, come to the opposite opinion. The Nurse is a "mumbling fool". She claims that "I speak no treason" because her actions in helping the marriage have been treasonous, and she wants to deny her guilt. She wants to deflect "blame", because Juliet could have married Paris if only the Nurse hadn't betrayed the Capulets by facilitating the marriage to Romeo.

10. "I think you are happy in this second match,
For it excels your first: or if it did not,
Your first is dead, or 'twere as good he were,
As living here and you no use of him."

The first two lines are longer than ten syllables, as the Nurse's pentameter breaks down. Shakespeare uses this device to show when something is wrong with what the character is saying. Here it portrays her advice as wrong. On a purely practical level, the Nurse's advice is very good. Now Romeo has killed Tybalt, there is no realistic expectation they will be able to make their marriage public. Marrying Paris is a better match socially and financially for Juliet, and a better alliance for her father. Romeo "is dead" because he cannot return to Verona, and also because Lady Capulet is going to hire an assassin to poison him. Her advice makes complete sense from a pragmatic point of view.

But it also betrays Juliet's love for Romeo. Much more damaging, to the Christian audience, is that it betrays Juliet's soul. If she marries while already married to Romeo, her soul will go to hell.

We could also argue that the Nurse's solution is a very adult one. Perhaps Shakespeare wants us to ask what we lose when we have left childhood. Do we become more corrupt and cynical? Does he want us to mourn our loss of childhood innocence?

Top Ten Mercutio Quotes

**1. "This is the hag, when maids lie on their backs,
That presses them and learns them first to bear".**

He likens this to "much misfortune". So, Mercutio's final point is that the worst tragedy of society is that women are forced to have children. This often leads to their own deaths, and the deaths of their children - Juliet is now an only child as her siblings have all been "swallowed up" and the Nurse's daughter Susan has also died young. Mercutio is therefore attacking the patriarchal control of women, and suggesting this is going to be a significant cause of Juliet's tragedy. Finally, he links this dreaming to "Quean" and "Mab". Both these words were Elizabethan slang for "whore". He's suggesting that all our dreams are corrupt, they all involve exploiting others but that the worst exploitation is the way society exploits women.

2. "Appear thou in likeness of a sigh, / Speak but one rhyme and I am satisfied, Cry but "Ay me," pronounce but "love" and "dove."

Mercutio is either the voice of cynicism or the voice of truth, depending on your viewpoint. He mocks Romeo's sense of himself as an unrequited lover as a pose. This seems an accurate portrayal of Romeo's seduction of Rosaline. He also mocks Romeo's poetry, with predictable rhymes like "love" and "dove". Both Romeo and Juliet use these words when speaking about love. In Mercutio's terms, this is evidence that their love is not real, but a confusion of sexual desire for love.

3. "Romeo, that she were, O, that she were / An open-arse, thou a poperin pear!"

Mercutio imagines Romeo's passion for Rosaline is intense sexual desire. Mercutio objectifies her as a "medlar" fruit because it is known as "An open-arse". Romeo is represented by the penis shaped fruit, the "poperin pear". Her identity, and indeed her face, are irrelevant to Romeo's passion – he simply wants to have sex with a woman. Anal sex is safe sex, and therefore leaves the female lover with her "flower", her virginity, which makes her so valuable in the marriage market.

Mercutio's natural images, of fruits, also imply that sexual desire is simply natural. We sense his frustration at the social rules around patriarchal marriage which make these desires so difficult to act upon.

Finally, his imagery of anal sex and Romeo's sexual desire also seems to indicate that Mercutio is imagining his own sexual desire for Romeo, and hoping that, if it is just the "open-arse" that matters to Romeo, then Mercutio might become his lover.

4. "thou hast more of the wild goose in one of thy wits than, I am sure, I have in my whole five."

Mercutio pretends to lose the battle of wits with Romeo. The "wild-goose" represents two things at once: it is a kind of horse race, and "goose" is slang for a prostitute. Mercutio pretends he has lost the horse race, which he is using as the metaphor for this battle of wits. When we hear his Queen Mab speech, or the quickfire jokes he makes as he is dying, we know that Mercutio would never lose a battle of wits. His real message to Romeo concerns the slang meaning of "goose". He's telling Romeo that he has very little desire for the "wild-goose" of chasing women, in comparison to Romeo.

This ratio of Romeo having more than "five" times this sexual desire for women is as close as he gets to a confession that his sexual desire is not for women, but for Romeo.

5. "Thou wilt quarrel with a man for cracking nuts, having no other reason but because thou hast hazel eyes."

Mercutio revels in conflict. We could say he turns every conversation into a conflict of some kind. Here he uses humour, as always, to portray Benvolio as seeking a "quarrel" at every opportunity. This is the opposite of the Benvolio we have seen in the play, permanently playing the role of peace keeper. Mercutio knows this about Benvolio, but he is trying to shape the world to his desires. We've seen how he wants Romeo to recognise his own sexual desire could be satisfied with Mercutio. Now, he wants a fight with the Capulets, and wants to persuade Benvolio, despite his request that they should "scape a brawl", that he actually wants to fight them.

6. "Consort? What, dost thou make us minstrels?"

A consort was a group of musicians playing the viol, a fiddle. But a consort was also the spouse of a king or queen. Both these descriptions suggest that Tybalt is attacking Mercutio's masculinity, and also insinuating that he is the equivalent of Romeo's wife. The final meaning of "consort" is that Tybalt is accusing Mercutio of playing together with Romeo, so not just suggesting that he is sexually attracted to Romeo, but that it is reciprocated and that they are lovers. There was no word for homosexuality in Elizabethan England. The idea that men would have erotic feelings for each other was not strange or uncommon. But it was seen as a private sexual experimentation which would need to be put aside with manhood and marriage. What angers Mercutio, then, is that Tybalt is making it public, and also that Romeo never seems to acknowledge or return Mercutio's desires.

7. "O calm, dishonourable, vile submission!"

Notice that Mercutio's first disgusted adjective is "calm". This indicates how much he loves conflict – "calm" is boring. He is also passionate about the same ideals of male honour as Tybalt, where reputation is everything. Not to stand up to a challenge to a duel is a "vile submission" because, in this male code, it means that you are admitting another man is more powerful than you are, even if their social rank is lower. Tybalt has a lower social rank than Romeo, and so it is inconceivable that Romeo should back down. To do so is "dishonourable".

So, why does Mercutio fight? He isn't going to restore Romeo's honour by duelling with Tybalt. He has at least two reasons. The first is that he hates "calm". The second is that he believes Tybalt will be easy to defeat because he has not learned to fight real opponents, instead he **"fights by the book of arithmetic"**. The ease with which Romeo later kills Tybalt also proves Mercutio was right.

8. Although Mercutio appears enraged enough to fight Tybalt, he has no intention of fighting a fatal duel. He makes this clear in advance to Tybalt, pointing out that he intends to draw only a little blood: **"Good King of Cats, nothing but one of your nine lives, that I mean to make bold withal, and, as you shall use me hereafter, dry-beat the rest of the eight."** He would need to take the other "eight" lives to kill Tybalt, and intends only to "dry-beat" them. He won't inflict further wounds which would, in contrast, be wet with blood.

9. "Ask for me to-morrow, and you / shall find me a grave man."

What's more important than death? Humour and bravery. These appear to be the two attributes which Mercutio values most. The double meaning of "grave" is brilliant. On one level it means serious. On another, he means that Romeo is the "man" who will have to find him "a grave".

We understand that he immediately recognises that his wound is fatal. Nevertheless, he is determined to die with style, panache and wit.

10. A plague o' both your houses. They have made worms' meat of me.

Mercutio's ending is a deliberate parallel of Romeo. Romeo refuses to accept responsibility for his actions, calling himself "fortune's fool". Similarly, Mercutio blames the feud for his death, rather than his impulsive need for "quarrel", a rejection of "calm" and a fear of seeming "dishonourable" in the masculine code of honour. We can't really say that Mercutio is a victim of the feud, nor even of that code of male honour. After all, defeating Tybalt himself would have done nothing to stop Romeo's "vile submission".

Shakespeare draws another parallel with Romeo, when Romeo sees Juliet in her tomb. Romeo tells her dead body, **"here will I remain / With worms that are thy chambermaids."** Mercutio's view of death is that there is no afterlife, the body is simply "meat". Romeo's romantic vision is that the "worms" will act as "chambermaids" to Juliet, making her even more beautiful, rather than reducing her to a skeleton.

Although Romeo's version ends the play, Mercutio's vision of the world throughout his scenes might appear more realistic. The counterpoint of their two visions of death might be intended to show us how misguided and pointless Romeo's suicide is.

Top Ten Tybalt Quotes

1. What, art thou drawn among these heartless hinds?
Turn thee Benvolio, look upon thy death.

There isn't really anything to like about Tybalt. He is unusual in the play, as there don't seem to be any conflicting aspects to his personality. He seems to represent a particular kind of manhood, obsessed with status, etiquette and violence to prove his worth. He embodies everything which was wrong with the masculine code of honour which included duelling as the ultimate expression of male prowess and status.

Shakespeare gives us his obsession with status when he dismisses the servants as "heartless hinds". Their status is conveyed through animal imagery, as deer, "hinds". Shakespeare also links the masculine code of honour to a patriarchal dismissal of women. So, Tybalt also chooses "hinds" because they are female deer.

He is also an interesting counterpoint to Romeo. Romeo's love poetry is used to suggest that he is playing at love, indulging in the pose of the unrequited lover made famous in Elizabethan England by Petrarch's sonnets. Tybalt's threats also feel like a pose. He describes himself as death, all powerful and unstoppable, when he tells Benvolio to "look upon thy death". This is ludicrous when framed with the childish bravado, sexual innuendo and thumb biting which precedes it.

2. "What, drawn, and talk of peace? I hate the word / As I hate hell, all Montagues, and thee."

Where Mercutio hates "calm", Tybalt hates "peace". This points to the main problem with the code of male honour. Whereas the elaborate etiquette around offence was intended, in Elizabethan times, to reduce violence, Shakespeare shows the opposite happens. If the consequence of a misplaced word is a duel to the death, then in theory all men become excessively courteous and polite. But in Shakespeare's version, young men seek out offence, and seek violence as a way of acquiring reputation.

By linking "hell" and "Montagues" Tybalt reveals that he believes his code of masculine honour is equivalent to a Christian code of behaviour. His hubris challenges God, as we shall see again later. He also appears to believe that he can defeat Benvolio, which we shall also see is probably hubris too.

In this quotation he breaks the iambic rhythm. This one begins with two stressed syllables (called a spondee). "Hate hell" is also a spondee. So, at his most boastful about the violence he wants to bring to Benvolio, he loses control of the iambic pentameter. This again suggest that his threat is forced, putting on a pose to sound much more dangerous than he is.

3. "Now by the stock and honour of my kin,
To strike him dead I hold it not a sin."

This is perhaps the turning point which leads to Tybalt's death. The previous two brawls (mentioned by the Prince) have involved some wounding, but no deaths. Despite his claims to embody "death" we can see that he is either not a skilled enough swordsman to kill his opponent, or he actually has no intent to kill.

But now he speaks in soliloquy. The convention is that characters speak their true thoughts, as their words are not chosen for others to hear. Up until now his "hate" has been directed generally at "all Montagues". Now he is focused only on killing Romeo.

This is also his moment of hubris, which causes his tragic fate. God would certainly call killing Romeo a sin, but Tybalt justifies murder to himself: "I hold it not a sin". This challenge to God is made because he instead worships "the stock and honour of my kin". The masculine attachment to "honour" and the family "feud" lead to Tybalt's tragic death.

4. "It fits when such a villain is a guest: / I'll not endure him."

Just as Romeo and Juliet might be mistaking sexual passion and the desire to rebel against their parents, for love, Tybalt is mistaking family "honour" for his own vanity and desire to prove himself through violence. If family "honour" were uppermost in his mind, he would not think to challenge Capulet at his own ball, instead he would defer to him because of his age and, even more importantly, because of his status as Lord.

5. "Patience perforce with wilful choler meeting
Makes my flesh tremble in their different greeting.
I will withdraw: but this intrusion shall,
Now seeming sweet, convert to bitter gall."

Speaking in couplets often signifies an ending. This happens with Tybalt making his exit, but his lines are also prophetic of Mercutio's and his own deaths. Again, the lines are a soliloquy, so we know this is not a pose to impress others and he intends to carry out his threat. Shakespeare dramatises this with two opposite forces fighting inside Tybalt, "patience" and anger - "choler" – from which he has a physical reaction, making his "flesh tremble". This conflict is also echoed in the pentameter, where "**Pa**tience **per**force" and "**Makes** my **flesh**" are both trochaic openings to the lines, before the last couplet returns to iambic meter. These four lines therefore mimic his conflict, with two contrasting couplets matching the two contrasting emotions.

If Tybalt is a counterpoint to Romeo, Shakespeare is asking us to consider what the two conflicting aspects of his character are. We will find out when he kills Tybalt – the "effeminate" lover, and the male killer. How annoying is that?

6. "Mercutio, thou consortest with Romeo."

We've learned that the Elizabethans had no word for homosexuality, and for a young man to have same sex relations was not considered unusual or sinful. However, it was seen as appropriate to the young. Once men matured, they were expected to marry and leave male lovers behind.

So then, as now, there was a tension between what constituted real masculinity. Because Tybalt is obsessed with male honour, the greatest insult he can throw at Romeo is that he and Mercutio are lovers. This is why he provokes Mercutio with the innuendo, "thou consortest with Romeo".

Ironically, this accusation doesn't anger Mercutio because he resents being thought of as Romeo's lover. His anger stems from not being Romeo's lover. Even a fool like Tybalt can see the homosexual overtones of Mercutio's relationship with Romeo, while Romeo seems totally oblivious.

7. "Romeo, the love I bear thee can afford
No better term than this: Thou art a villain."

Because Tybalt is so obsessed with status, he believes that calling Romeo, who is the son of a Lord, a lowly born "villain" will provoke him into a duel. Romeo of course is not provoked, because he is now Tybalt's kinsman by marriage. Unfortunately, Tybalt has contrasted this insult with the word "love". This is unfortunate, because Romeo picks it up as a theme, repeatedly telling Tybalt that he has a "reason" to "love" him.

This enrages Tybalt, because the homosexual slur he tried to provoke Mercutio with has now been aimed at him. Because he believes in the sexual relationship between Romeo and Mercutio, Tybalt is horrified at the implication that Romeo might find him attractive.

But what might the effect of Romeo's declaration of "love" be on Mercutio? He is also enraged that Romeo uses this love to back down from his masculine duty to duel with Tybalt. Part of that rage could well be that he is expressing affection for Tybalt, as well as showing apparent cowardice in not fighting. It is these conflicting emotions which lead him to challenge Tybalt who, as we saw from his soliloquy, is only interested in killing Romeo.

8. "Tybalt, the reason that I have to love thee
Doth much excuse the appertaining rage
To such a greeting."

The homosexual overtones of Tybalt's and Mercutio's quarrel leads to the tragedy of Mercutio's death. Tybalt has never killed anyone before - his duels have been ritualised. This is why he has written to Romeo to make a formal challenge. It is why he can't simply draw his sword and fight Romeo now, he needs Romeo to verbally accept the challenge, otherwise the attack would be dishonourable and unmanly. Not only does he call Romeo a "villain", but he also hints at his erotic desire for Mercutio. This is why he contrasts "the love I bear thee" with Mercutio's love.

"Boy, this shall not excuse the injuries / That thou hast done me, therefore turn and draw." The social convention of masculine honour is that Romeo has to answer the challenge. Remember, Tybalt issued this as formally as possible, in a letter sent to Romeo's father's house. He simply can't believe that Romeo is backing down, when social etiquette says he must fight to restore his honour.
In a last attempt to force him into a duel, he calls Romeo a "boy", as an attack on his manhood. Shakespeare mocks this etiquette which requires duelling through Mercutio's description of Tybalt as a "butcher of a silk button", and he mocks it again here when Tybalt says why he wants to fight. It is because of "the injuries That thou hast done me". Well, there have been no injuries. There have not even been any insults – by attending the Capulet ball, he has injured only Capulet. But Tybalt is so full of his own vanity that he takes this as a personal affront.

The etiquette of the duel also traps Tybalt's anger. If Romeo does not "turn and draw", Tybalt cannot attack him.

9. "I was hurt under your arm." ✓ cheat

Tybalt breaks with his code of honour when he stabs Mercutio who was stabbed "under your [Romeo's] arm". Mercutio blames Romeo. But in terms of the code of honour Tybalt lives by, he should never take advantage of Romeo's intervention. Perhaps we can read in to this how much rage he is feeling as a result of misunderstanding Romeo's declaration of love for him.

10. "Thou wretched boy, that didst consort him here, / Shalt with him hence."

Tybalt returns. Perhaps he feels that he has failed a test of honour, and the only way to restore his reputation is to fight again - this time fairly. This is his hubris, believing that he is able to kill Romeo. Remember, he has not manged to kill a Montague in any of the brawls which "thrice" gave him the opportunity. He was unable even to injure Benvolio in the duel he demanded at the beginning of the play. Mercutio's claim that he fights like someone who has just learned a pattern of moves like "pricksong", that he "fights by the book of arithmetic" is proved correct. Romeo appears to kill him easily, and certainly escapes uncut himself.

Tybalt's ending is one sided. He is given hardly any lines compared to Romeo, and his final line is cut short at 4 syllables and finished by Romeo with 6 syllables. Shakespeare contrasts this with the verbal flourishes and metaphors and humour of Mercutio's final words. This is a clear message that we should dismiss Tybalt and the male honour he represents.

His final insults to Romeo are unoriginal. Calling him a "boy" is less insulting than his earlier "villain". Perhaps he wants to intimidate Romeo by pointing out that he, Tybalt, is a man in comparison to Romeo who is like a child. Then he repeats the accusation that Romeo and Mercutio were lovers "that didst consort", but this too has no effect on Romeo.

As usual there are no stage directions to help us picture the duel. If Shakespeare wants to extend a fight, such as the fight between Macbeth and Macduff in the play Macbeth, he gives the characters dialogue during the fight. Tybalt is silenced, and we can infer Romeo defeats him quickly.

This speed and ease of victory also suggests that Mercutio was right, Tybalt's skill as a "duellist" was simply a pose, a threat only to "a silk button". He has died because of his hubris and arrogance and his hamartia has been the belief in male and family honour. The final irony is Capulet's reaction to his death, as head of the family he died for. Rather than praise him as a heroic or noble figure, he simply dismisses his death with **"Well, we were born to die."** Ultimately Shakespeare dismisses Tybalt and his views as irrelevant.

Top Ten Friar Quotes

**1. "For naught so vile that on the earth doth live
But to the earth some special good doth give;"**

Shakespeare wants his audience to have conflicted feelings about the Friar. First, he represents the Catholic church, which was suppressed in Elizabethan England. Secondly, in the source poem, he is clearly blamed for the marriage and the tragedy, without redeeming features. Shakespeare wants his audience to understand the Friar's motivation. In this first introduction to him we get the essential exposition that he is an expert herbalist – this will be essential in understanding his ability to produce a potion that will mimic death.

But this couplet and his soliloquy also reveal his philosophy, wanting to extract "special good" from things which might seem "so vile". This perfectly explains why he will decide to risk performing the secret marriage.

He also repeats "the earth", which perhaps reveals his concern for the living, rather than the more abstract idea of the eternal life of the soul. He is a healer, focused on helping the living and alleviating their suffering.

**2. "Thy love did read by rote, that could not spell.
But come young waverer, come go with me,
In one respect I'll thy assistant be;
For this alliance may so happy prove,
To turn your households' rancour to pure love."**

Shakespeare often uses the Friar as the voice of wisdom. Even though we criticise his decisions, his view of characters and the world usually feels wise. When he says Romeo's "love did read by rote" we believe him, and we share his worries that his love for Juliet is not real. When he calls Romeo "young waverer" we also wonder if the suddenness of his marriage to Juliet is also too quick.

But he suddenly ignores his own misgivings in order to try to end "households' rancour" between the feuding families. We can see that this ambition is noble, as he wants to replace the "rancour" with "pure love". We can infer that he sees his decision as "pure", even though it is deceitful and dangerous.

There is an added barrier to our simply dismissing him as deluded, which we learn in the Prologue that the marriage is "star-crossed" and "death-marked", meaning Fate has chosen their death. But then we find out Fate's purpose: **"And the continuance of their parents' rage, / Which, but their children's end, nought could remove"**. This implies their death is part of God's plan. We can at least imagine that the Friar believes he is acting for good and a noble cause when he marries them, even if the audience will disapprove of the betrayal of the parents.

3. "Wisely and slow. They stumble that run fast."

Here again Shakespeare contrasts the adult and youthful worlds. The Friar associates wisdom with being "slow", whereas youth wants to "run fast". The adult perspective is that this speed will lead to a "stumble", whereas to the young such speed is closer to freedom and the ability to be oneself rather than be held back by slowness. The marriage, as the lovers see it, is freedom from patriarchal parental control and freedom to choose whom they love and marry.

Shakespeare also makes these words ironic. If the Friar followed his own advice, he too would move much more slowly in arranging the marriage and in formulating the plan to help Juliet escape by mimicking death.

4. "These violent delights have violent ends,
And in their triumph die; like fire and powder,
Which as they kiss consume. The sweetest honey
Is loathsome in his own deliciousness,"

The Friar uses imagery which is also prophetic, so we can hear how he brings about the tragedy, while he is oblivious to this (as he doesn't know how the lovers end). He calls their passion for each other "violent delights", linking love and death as the lovers do themselves. He foresees "violent ends", and presumably means a sudden end to their love for each other once real life and time spent together get in the way. We hear, instead, the "violent ends" of their deaths. His adult perspective is that "The sweetest honey" has to be had in moderation – too much will make it "loathsome". His language predicts that their love, so intense now, will burn itself out over time "like fire and powder". He is warning the lovers that their love feels real, but the sheer intensity of what they are feeling is proof that it cannot last.

The Friar's adult tone is measured. Just as he showed his belief in balance between the good and dangerous properties of herbs, so he sees a need to balance elements of life. This was an Elizabethan view, which saw mental and physical health being controlled by balance in the four humours. These humours are liquids in the body (blood, yellow bile, black bile, phlegm) and an imbalance in each one caused anger, happiness, depression etc. This fact means that the audience are already primed to agree with the Friar.

Perhaps Romeo and Juliet's attraction to death solves this problem. They will die before the extreme passion of their love cools and settles into the adult world view shared by the Friar and much of Shakespeare's audience.

5. "A lover may bestride the gossamers
That idles in the wanton summer air,
And yet not fall. So light is vanity."

Friar Lawrence says this as he sees Juliet arrive. He portrays life as a trap, like a spider's web. Here, the trap isn't that the web is sticky, but that it is so thin. The lover believes she can "bestride the gossamer" thin fibres of the web "And yet not fall". But this is the youthful view – the Friar's adult view is that the "fall" is inevitable. He calls Juliet's belief in the power of love to achieve the impossible "vanity". It is impossible to walk on a web, and it is impossible for the power of their love to survive into adult life. To believe otherwise, he says, is arrogant pride – "vanity" in this quotation, and hubris in the world of tragedy.

Why does he tell the lovers these warnings? Well, he is preparing them for the disappointments to come. The tragedy might be that the lovers believe him, and this makes their decision to reject adulthood easier. Perhaps he makes death more attractive than age and adulthood.

6. "For by your leaves, you shall not stay alone,
Til Holy Church incorporate two in one."

One way of analysing the play is to consider it from the point of view of the adult world and the world of youth. Benvolio, the Friar, the Nurse, the Capulet and Montague parents have an adult perspective, which is pragmatic, practical, not prone to fantasy and belief in romantic love. Then we have Mercutio, Tybalt and Romeo who adopt roles and poses, rebel against authority and indulge in fantasy. Then Juliet straddles these two worlds – she is fully aware of the adult world and the practical sacrifices women have to make in it, but she also believes in love, escape and the fantasy that she and Romeo can be united in death, or at least believes she will be happier dead than alive without Romeo.

Shakespeare forces us to question which view, the adult or the youthful perspective, has more value. Here, the Friar is so convinced that Romeo and Juliet are motivated by a desperate sexual desire, that he refuses to let them "stay alone" together until they are married. He believes that they are so desperate to have sex that they will do so in church while he is preparing the marriage service. Well, is he right? It forces us to consider how much each lover is motivated by sexual desire, rather than a love we can believe in. It also makes us wonder how the rules of the adult world force the lovers to marry before they can have sex. Shakespeare's own marriage, where Anne was already three months pregnant suggests that he might not have believed in this patriarchal control of women as virgins till their wedding day. At 18, with a 26-year-old wife, it is quite likely that she was not a virgin before she met Shakespeare.

7. "Hold, daughter. I do spy a kind of hope,
Which craves as desperate an execution
As that is desperate which we would prevent."

An interesting way to understand the role of the Friar is to see him as the counterpoint to Capulet. He calls Juliet "daughter" and he plays the role in society of "father". Like Capulet, he treats Juliet as an object. He takes a huge risk in giving her a "liquor" which will mimic death and, if the dosage is wrong, actually result in death. We can argue in his defence that he believes her threat to commit suicide, and so this is a far better solution despite the risk. But as we will see, he doesn't believe in her threat. Instead, he is protecting his own interests – the solution will remove Juliet from Verona in such a way that his role in marrying them will never be exposed. He sees that, now Romeo has killed Tybalt, the Friar's plan to unite the families is now hopeless. Capulet makes the same kind of decision in disposing of Juliet for his own interests.

As usual, Shakespeare uses irony. The Friar's "desperate...execution" leads to the desperate executions of the lovers at their own hands. This language is a way for Shakespeare to emphasise the Friar's culpability.

8. "If no inconstant toy, nor womanish fear, / Abate thy valour in the acting it."

I've chosen this quotation because it proves that the Friar didn't really believe that Juliet would commit suicide. If he did, there would be no need to worry about "womanish fear" to drink the "liquor" which imitates death. It also reveals his patriarchal prejudice against women, as having insufficient "valour" and being full of "womanish fear". He also assumes she could be easily distracted with other ideas, which he portrays as an "inconstant toy". We can interpret this as a lack of respect for Juliet, which is also dismissive. Again, we recognise the same qualities in Capulet.

9. "The most you sought was her promotion,
For 'twas your heaven she should be advanc'd,
And weep ye now, seeing she is advanc'd
Above the clouds, as high as heaven itself?"

The Friar's reaction to the Capulets is quite brutal. They have discovered Juliet's apparently dead body, and instead of allowing the parents their grief, he attacks their faith and their motives. He accuses them of placing their faith in social advancement, which became their "heaven". He contrasts this with how God has "advanc'd" her to "heaven itself".

What motivates him to say this? Perhaps it is anger at the patriarchal society which normalises now fathers can trade their daughters for "promotion". The Friar sees himself as different. The marriage is for the greater good of both families, producing "pure love" and peace. Perhaps he also feels that, even though their love is full of "violent passions", it will be a better marriage than the one to Paris. This is a genuine point of difference between the two men even though we can argue they are equally manipulative of Juliet.

10. "Come, I'll dispose of thee/ Among a sisterhood of holy nuns."

At the end of the play the Friar reveals himself as a coward. He flees, rather than being caught with Juliet and the corpses of Romeo and Paris. But before he makes that decision, he offers Juliet his final solution. Rather than confess his part in the marriage and his plan to drug Juliet to pretend that she is dead, he is going to get rid of her. He says "I'll dispose of thee". This language is extremely callous. He isn't offering to help her escape, or to help her hide from her family – his words reveal that he is treating her, and her future, as refuse, something to be thrown away, disposed of.

Although she is religious, we can imagine Juliet is not attracted to living with "holy nuns" as a nun herself. There is the possibility that the Friar is counting on her horrified refusal to come with him, leaving her so horrified at this loveless future that she would rather kill herself. We can't prove that of course, but there is a telling detail when he confesses everything to the Prince. He doesn't say he suggested Juliet should come to a nunnery, instead he claims to have told her to **"come forth / And bear this work of heaven with patience"**. What reason can he have to lie? It is to cover his guilt at the offer he made her? That implies it contributed to her suicide.

Astonishingly, the Prince simply accepts that all of the Friar's motives have been good, including the decision to marry Romeo and Juliet. He says despite everything, **"We still have known thee for a holy man."**

Shakespeare does not tell us what to think of the Friar's skilful manipulation and motives and whether he really is a better "father" to Juliet than Capulet. We must decide for ourselves.

Top Ten Benvolio Quotes

1. "Part, fools! put up your swords, you know not what you do."

Benvolio acts as the voice of reason. An interesting way of looking at him is by contrasting him with the wildly impulsive Mercutio. If you get a question on Mercutio, he is likely to be contrasted with Tybalt, but I see Benvolio and Mercutio as the two contrasting halves of Romeo's character.

Here, he is trying to diffuse the feud, even before the Prince intervenes. His voice comes from the adult perspective, like Friar Lawrence, who also wants to end the feud. When he tells the fighters "you know not what you do", he is asking them to think about the consequences of their actions.

It is probably true to say that Benvolio is the only character who properly thinks through the consequences of what they do, while all the rest are persuaded by hubris that consequences will be in their favour, no matter what risk they are taking.

2. "A troubled mind drave me to walk abroad,
Where underneath the grove of sycamore
That westward rooteth from this city side,
So early walking did I see your son."

Benvolio suffers from a melancholic "humour", just like Romeo. However, Romeo's life is upside down, staying up all night, then returning home to hide from his parents. Benvolio's "troubled mind" wakes him up just before dawn. The sibilance of the last two lines suggests a peacefulness he has found, in contrast to the turmoil of Romeo's unrequited love. He is, perhaps, a mature version of Romeo's immaturity.

3. "Take thou some new infection to thy eye,
And the rank poison of the old will die."

Benvolio also takes the opposite view of love to Romeo. He sees the emotions of being in love as an "infection", because it alters the personality. This is also Mercutio's objection. Like the Friar, he sees that the lover simply falls in love with beauty, rather than personality or inherent worth, so it is an **"infection to the eye".**

When love is unrequited, that "infection" becomes a "rank poison". He proposes the solution to this is simply to find a more attractive woman to fall in love with, presumably until eventually he might find one who returns his affections. In Mercutio, this description of love would feel cynical. But because Shakespeare has taken the trouble to present Benvolio as the mature peace maker, trusted by Romeo's parents, he asks us to consider if his view of young male love is also a mature perspective.

4. "Compare her face with some that I shall show, / And I will make thee think thy swan a crow."

Shakespeare gives Benvolio a rhyming couplet, which also has the effect of making his words appear wise. The sibilance in the first line and the alliteration and contrast of the second also makes this seem well thought out and accomplished.

He also introduces the black and white imagery which Romeo uses when he sees Juliet. They both focus on other women as "crows", and Romeo replaces the "swan" which represents Rosaline, to the "dove" which represents Juliet.

Shakespeare may do this to show the irony of Benvolio's cure. Exactly what he predicts comes to pass, even the way Romeo thinks about beauty is controlled by Benvolio's imagery. Unfortunately, in being right, he sets in motion the tragedy.

5. "The date is out of such prolixity: We'll have no Cupid hoodwink'd with a scarf,"

Benvolio simply understands the adult world best, and takes charge. Romeo wants to know if they need a speech prepared for when they are announced, but Benvolio knows this is out of fashion, telling us "the date is out".

Then he mocks Romeo's obsession with love, saying "we'll have no Cupid", meaning a boy dressed up as Cupid to announce their arrival as young, desirable men, looking for love. He then introduces the imagery of falconry which Romeo and Juliet will both pick up later, when he imagines "Cupid hoodwink'd". This blindfold changes Cupid to represents his blindness. This is again prophetic – both lovers will find each other, blind to their conflicting family names. But their love will also be blind to the consequences of their marriage.

Shakespeare uses this imagery to make us ask if their love is blind, or whether knowing their love is forbidden makes them more attracted to each other.

6. "Blind is his love, and best befits the dark."

Benvolio continues this imagery when talking to Mercutio. He imagines Romeo's love is "blind" because he simply sees that Rosaline is not that attractive – she is a "crow", rather than the "swan" Romeo thinks she is.

The alliteration also implies an element of disgust that Romeo is in "the dark" because he is so blind. A further possibility is the Benvolio also means that whomever Romeo loves will also be a "blind" choice, made without rational thought. Although he represents the adult perspective, Benvolio is the youngest character who does so. Perhaps he is offered up as the model of what Romeo could have been, had he not been so impulsive and desperate for love.

7. "I pray thee, good Mercutio, let's retire: The day is hot, the Capulets abroad, And if we meet, we shall not scape a brawl, For now these hot days, is the mad blood stirring."

Benvolio can sense trouble before it happens. He knows that heat leads to violence, so points out "The day is hot". He knows that murder and violence increase on very hot days (which is actually true). He also knows that the Capulets are "abroad", looking for "a brawl" and they will be agitated by "mad blood". He is desperate to save Mercutio from himself. After all, he could simply leave and avoid confrontation, but he wants to take Mercutio with him. Although Mercutio is not a target, as he is not a Montague, he also senses that Mercutio is just as likely to provoke the brawl himself.

Once again, Benvolio is the adult voice of reason, and once again he is ignored by his youthful friends.

8. "We talk here in the public haunt of men.
Either withdraw unto some private place,
And reason coldly of your grievances,
Or else depart; here all eyes gaze on us."

Once Mercutio draws his sword, ready to fight Tybalt, Benvolio intervenes. He tries to reframe the duel by pointing out "we talk", which is a subtle way of de-escalating. He points out that this is a "public" place, to help them remember the Prince's promised punishment to further public brawls. He describes it as a "haunt of men" which carries the connotation of death through "haunt", subtly reminding them of the consequences of fighting. He contrasts the heat of the day which he warned about with what they should do, "reason coldly", without violence.

But, because his voice represents the adult world, it is ignored by Mercutio and Tybalt.

9. "BENVOLIO: Hence, be gone, away!
ROMEO: O, I am fortune's fool!
BENVOLIO: Why dost thou stay?"

Although Romeo tries to think like an adult once he is married, and tries to stop the fight between Mercutio and Tybalt, he does not think through the consequence of doing so. So, Romeo intervenes, puts himself between Mercutio and Tybalt, and Mercutio is stabbed and killed under Romeo's arm. Though Romeo asks Benvolio to stop the fight, he knows it is too risky, and does not.

Now that Romeo has killed Tybalt, we find again that he has not thought through the consequences. So, Benvolio has a couplet to tell him to "be gone, away" and then to force him out of his inaction. He completely ignores Romeo's attempt to pass the blame on to "fortune", sandwiching it between his rhyming couplet. In this way Shakespeare emphasises the superiority of Benvolio's thinking compared to Romeo.

10. "And as he fell did Romeo turn and fly.
This is the truth, or let Benvolio die."

Unlike the Friar at the end of the play, Benvolio's narrative is totally truthful. The Prince takes everything he says at face value, and is then able to justify banishing Romeo rather than executing him. We could argue that Benvolio's plausibility saves Romeo's life. In many ways he is the male role model in the play. Because of this, his last words occur in Act 3 Scene 1. Shakespeare simply removes him from the tragedy, to preserve him from the chaos that follows. This removal can be read as an endorsement of Benvolio's point of view. Only the characters who have not thought through the consequences of their actions feature in the remaining acts.

Top Ten Capulet Quotes

1. "She hath not seen the change of fourteen years;
Let two more summers wither in their pride
Ere we may think her ripe to be a bride."

We have strong reasons for believing the play is an attack on masculinity in Shakespeare's day. Remember why he starts with sexual bravado before the fight at the start, and remember Tybalt's obsession with "honour", and finally remember what triggers the rushed marriage isn't just love, it is Juliet's need to escape the proposed match to Paris.

To best dramatise patriarchal injustice, Shakespeare creates Capulet. Remember that the decision to marry Paris after Tybalt's death was originally, in Brooke's poem, Lady Capulet's idea. This didn't suit Shakespeare, who wanted it to be a father's, and therefore a male's decision.

Here we see him being apparently reasonable, asking Paris to wait "two more summers" before marrying Juliet. True, Juliet will still be sixteen and therefore very young, but that is still significantly different from being not yet "fourteen". And let's weigh up what he stands to gain – a very rich and influential groom who will boost his own family's fortunes by boosting his political influence, because Paris is a Count and is related to the Prince. This alliance will also strengthen his position in the feud with the Montagues. Now, asking Paris to wait two years is a real risk. As such an influential bachelor, he can have his pick of brides from more eager fathers. So, we really do get a sense of Capulet trying to do the best for his daughter within a patriarchal system which treats women as saleable assets, to be sold when they have most value, as young, beautiful virgins.

Next, we have to consider how he describes her at sixteen, "we think her ripe to be a bride". This language of harvest objectifies her. It embodies the idea that she must be sold at the right time, like a ripened fruit. "Ripe" is also a sensual adjective. It invites Paris to think about colour, texture and taste. The metaphor suggests that Juliet is being grown to be both consumed by a man, to satisfy his appetite and bring him pleasure. So, even in the best-case scenario, Capulet still thinks of his daughter as an asset to be traded or sold when the time is right.

2. "And too soon marr'd are those so early made.
The earth hath swallowed all my hopes but she,
She is the hopeful lady of my earth:
But woo her, gentle Paris, get her heart,
My will to her consent is but a part;"

This exposition gives us so much detail about Juliet's upbringing and Capulet's experience of parenthood and marriage. His warns that making Juliet a mother "so early" would "mar" her, but he doesn't speak specifically about her, instead he generalises. This prompts us to think that he is talking from experience, especially as Shakespeare makes sure we know that Lady Capulet gave birth too Juliet when she was thirteen. The formal relationship between mother and daughter which Shakespeare contrasts to Juliet and the Nurse, supports our conclusion that Lady Capulet's young age prevented her becoming a nurturing mother.

Then we find out that Juliet had more siblings, but they all died. Capulet's choice of metaphor, describing these children as "hopes" may be paternal, or may signify that he thought of them as commodities, like Juliet, that he had hopes of benefiting from them when they were "ripe". He describes Juliet as his "hopeful lady". Because "lady" is also used as a title for the wife of a lord, we can infer that Capulet has indeed thought of all his children as commodities like her, whom he can marry into noble families.

Next, he states that Juliet will have some say in the marriage, that he will ask for "her consent" and that he would like Paris to "woo her" and cause Juliet's "heart" to fall in love with him. If we take this at face value, we feel he is doing his best for his daughter. It suggests he looks back at his wife's experience and realises it was unjust and has damaged her. He asks Paris to be "gentle", because he fears that Paris wants Juliet to become a "mother" straight away.

3. "Content thee, gentle coz, let him alone,
A bears him like a portly gentleman;
And, to say truth, Verona brags of him
To be a virtuous and well-govern'd youth."

Capulet continues to appear reasonable at his ball. This is a momentous occasion, given that he has not attended one in about thirty years. These are huge social events which emphasise the host's wealth and influence. Hosting Paris is also an opportunity to show off his growing political influence.

We also get the impression that he has listened to the Prince's warning, and would much rather keep the peace and eject Romeo. More than that, he takes a very balanced view of his enemy's son, facing the object "truth" of Romeo's reputation as "virtuous" and "well-governed". It seems that Capulet represents the same reasonable adult perspective as the Friar.

4. "Things have fallen out, sir, so unluckily
That we have had no time to move our daughter.
Look you, she lov'd her kinsman Tybalt dearly,
And so did I. Well, we were born to die."

Capulet's true nature comes when he is under pressure. Paris uses Tybalt's death to his tactical advantage. He keeps pressing Capulet to let him marry Juliet. This is more important now – Tybalt is Capulet's brother's son, so his extended family is now weaker in the feud with the Montagues. Paris has completely dismissed Capulet's idea that he should wait till Juliet is sixteen, and Capulet has stopped protesting. He just asks for some "time to move" Juliet. But then he changes his mind instantly because of Tybalt's death. He claims he loved "Tybalt dearly" which seems to contradict their relationship at the ball. Then he immediately tells Paris, "Well, we were born to die". The obvious interpretation of this is that he didn't love Tybalt at all, and is callously happy to move on and get on with life. But a deeper meaning is that his observation is true. Remember how all his children have died, except for Juliet. She too is "born to die", and if that happens soon, it leaves him without an asset to trade. Part of him is probably thinking about the risk of not marrying her off while he has the chance. This lack of emotion and sympathy suggests that Capulet's early, reasonable manner was just a pose, a thin veneer which is stripped away when circumstances become difficult.

5. "How now? A conduit, girl? What, still in tears?

Evermore showering? In one little body
Thou counterfeits a bark, a sea, a wind."

Tybalt was only killed the day before. Capulet responds to his daughter's grief without empathy, but also with outright scorn and disgust. We are shocked at his complaint that she is "still in tears" because, even if she weren't married to Romeo, tears after one day of grief are very reasonable. Next, he accuses her of attention seeking, dramatising her grief unnecessarily. This idea of faking is conveyed by "Thou counterfeits". He calls her tears a fountain – "a conduit" – and then suggests that her body has become both a boat – "a bark" – tossed on a stormy sea, and the actual "sea" and "wind" that tosses it. Again, this emphasises how he feels her emotions are unreal and faked. This extreme reaction suggests that he both has no empathy, but also that he rejects emotion. In this sense he is a mixture of the worst masculine qualities.

Shakespeare also uses this contrast to show what patriarchal society does to men. It doesn't just damage women who are exploited. The need for men to compete and gain advantage leads to this lack of emotion and empathy in older men, just as it leads to sexual bravado and violence in the younger men or teenage boys.

6. "But fettle your fine joints 'gainst Thursday next
To go with Paris to Saint Peter's Church,
Or I will drag thee on a hurdle thither.
Out, you green-sickness carrion! Out, you baggage!
You tallow-face!"

In this insult we can see that Capulet sees his daughter entirely as bred for sex and reproduction. The metaphor of her having "fine joints" comes from pottery, as he wants to mould her entirely to his and Paris's desires. Focusing on her "joints" also invites her to think about her hip girdle. The choice of verb, "fettle" continues the pottery metaphor, but is also chosen for the fricative alliteration. This repetition of "f" clearly has sexual overtones here. It is a clue that he sees his daughter's sexuality as being the lure to attract Paris as a suitor.

Being dragged in public on "a hurdle" was a punishment for traitors. Just as a traitor would be tortured and then executed, Capulet intends to torture her with insults. These are revealing – he sees her as dead meat, "carrion", because until she marries he gets nothing in exchange for her. She is "baggage" because her worth is only measured in what she can bring to him through marriage – without the marriage, she is simply occupying space. All these metaphors point to her proper role in the patriarchal marriage, to enrich her parents through an advantageous alliance.

Capulet's disgust at Juliet's refusal at the match with Paris reflects the violence of patriarchal society towards women. Although he appears entirely unreasonable and "too hot" with rage, much of what he says is exactly how the patriarchal society deals with women.

Patriarchal society would view a noble daughter's refusal to marry as betraying the family's interests. Her only hope then would be to join a convent as a nun. Capulet's invective sounds very violent, but when he says "my fingers itch" he means he wants to hit her, but resists. After all, he needs to send her unblemished to her wedding. He does give her an alternative to obeying him, which is to "Graze where you will". Here "graze" marks her out as a farm animal, which emphasises her patriarchal duty to breed. Shakespeare is dramatising the exact predicament of a noble woman in Elizabethan

England. Interestingly, the Elizabethan era saw changing social attitudes to marriage. It is entirely conceivable that Shakespeare and Anne arranged pregnancy to force the families to allow their marriage. Women and men from low social status families would be much more likely to marry for love. But wealthy families concerned with increasing wealth, inheritance and influence would not. So, it is very possible that Shakespeare wants his audience to sympathy with the wealthy women who in terms of marriage have less freedom than they do.

7. "To have her match' d, and having now provided
A gentleman of noble parentage,
Of fair demesnes, youthful, and nobly allied,
Stuff'd, as they say, with honourable parts,"

Capulet justifies his anger in a way which many noble men might agree with. Shakespeare does that to challenge that part of his audience, as Capulet's reaction clearly prompts Juliet to consider suicide. He voices the patriarchal view that the "match" to Paris is exceptional. Not only is Paris "of noble parentage", he is also attractive – "fair"- and "youthful". By the standards of the day, this is very rare. Capulet hasn't been to a masked ball with his cousin in about thirty years, so he is probably nearly fifty years old. Lady Capulet gave birth to Juliet at thirteen, so is only twenty-six. When she married, Capulet was probably at least thirty years old.

So, Capulet sees that the husband he has chosen for Juliet proves what a considerate and skilled father he is. This pride makes it more shocking for him when Juliet refuses to marry Paris in such a dramatic way. Given the terms of patriarchal control, her refusal seems like a madness he can't understand.

Although we are supposed to understand Capulet's rage, Shakespeare has framed it so that we reject this patriarchal view of daughters. We aren't just appalled at him, but at the social system which treats women as possessions.

8. "Ay, you have been a mouse-hunt in your time".

This metaphor characterises Capulet as a cat, and the "mouse-hunt" as pursuing women. It is casually dropped into conversation, as though this behaviour is totally normal for a husband. The implication is that he has only stopped because of his age and even his wealth is not enough to make him attractive to young women. A further implication is that wives simply have to put up with this. Capulet is simply delighted that his wife has brought it up. He sees it as proof that she loves him, and is jealous of the women he as sex with: "A jealous hood, a jealous hood!" We are reminded that both Romeo and Juliet focused on the word "faithful" when they made their vows love to each other. They aren't just rebelling against their parents because that's what teenage children do - they are rebelling against a corrupt and oppressive system they find immoral. How their parents' generation treats marriage and the rights of wives and daughters is what disgusts them most.

"A jealous-hood, a jealous-hood!"

I include this because it reveals that Capulet has been repeatedly unfaithful. It implies that sex with his incredibly young wife has been entirely about reproduction, whereas for sexual pleasure he has had affairs with women, rather than girls. This is a treble attack on the patriarchal system. Firstly, it shows how girls are forced into reproduction before their bodies are really ready for sex, never mind childbirth. Secondly, it shows the hypocrisy of marriage in contrast to the "faithful" declarations of Romeo and Juliet. In this society, husbands do not expect to have to be faithful to their wives. But thirdly, a husband's affairs are common knowledge – he doesn't even hide them from his wife. He is delighted that his wife might have been "jealous" because he sees that as proof of her lover for him, rather than disappointment at his lack of love or respect.

Although Capulet is a deeply unsympathetic character, we shouldn't see him as an example of a terrible father who drives his loving daughter to suicide. Shakespeare is asking his audience about patriarchal fathers in London society: is their thinking any different to Capulet's?

9. "son, the night before thy wedding day
Hath death lain with thy bride. There she lies,
Flower as she was, deflowered by him."

Even Capulet's grief disgusts us. When he tells Paris that Juliet is dead, he uses the only metaphor he can think of which will reveal the right level of pain. So, he personifies "death" as a lover who has taken Juliet's virginity, her "flower". Death has "lain with" her before she could become Paris's "bride". Death is personified as a male rival, who has proved more powerful than Paris. The pain of sexual betrayal, especially around a wife's virginity, is as great as the pain of losing a bride through death. This is extra-ordinary, and shows the ridiculous value placed on controlling a woman's sexuality.

Shakespeare uses Capulet to help us understand how oppressive this must be for Juliet, and why she is desperate to have sex on her own terms, with a husband she is in love with. It is interesting that Juliet sees sex as an experience of shared enjoyment, and doesn't attach significance to Romeo being able to "deflower" her. She expects him to value her for herself, not because she is a virgin, and not because she can carry his babies and provide him heirs.

Shakespeare also adds irony to the image - Juliet has lost her virginity to Romeo, and when she lay with him, she lay with "death". It was her marriage to Romeo that has led to her taking the drug, and will lead to Romeo drinking his own poison, which will lead to Juliet's actual death.

10. "brother Montague, give me thy hand. / This is my daughter's jointure, for no more Can I demand."

The play ends with the families making peace. This solves the feud, but still leaves all the problems which caused the tragedy – the patriarchal control of women – firmly in place. The "jointure" is the part of a dowry paid over should either spouse die. Capulet's payment is peace, symbolised by "give me thy hand". Even in grief, they still talk about their dead children in financial terms, and then extend this with promises to build "golden" statues of each other's dead children.

Romeo has just spoken the same words, "give me thy hand" to Paris's corpse, as he has taken Paris's hand to drag him into the tomb near Juliet. We can imagine how horrified Juliet might have been at this gesture, but honour between men triumphs over loyalty between men and women.

1. "This is the matter. Nurse, give leave awhile,
We must talk in secret. Nurse, come back again,"

Shakespeare presents Juliet's mother as a remote figure. She seems to have passed all the nurturing parts of motherhood to the Nurse, who even sleeps in the same room as Juliet. Lady Capulet is also obsessed with status. Shakespeare suggests this is because of the circumstances of her marriage, where she was twelve and Juliet's father at least thirty. Her whole life was therefore traded by her own father so that she could marry a "rich Capulet", who is also a lord.

Here she insists that the nurse leave while she tells Juliet about the proposed marriage to Paris. The Nurse is a servant and therefore should not be privy to this conversation. Immediately, and in order to explain to the Elizabethan audience the importance of the Nurse, she breaks with this social etiquette, and asks her servant to remain. She knows the Nurse will be instrumental in persuading Juliet to marry Paris, and so heeds her present.

2. "Tell me, daughter Juliet,
How stands your disposition to be married?"

Lady Capulet's insistence on her status is reflected in her very formal and cold language. She doesn't even use Juliet's name, because this would imply both familiarity and an acknowledgement that Juliet has her own inner life. Lady Capulet is much more interested in Juliet as a "daughter" who has a duty to respect her parents, both because they are parents, and because they are a noble lord and lady. When she asks this question in such a formal way it feels less like a question, and more like a request or instruction that she ought to have a "disposition to be married".

Juliet is instantly wary and lies to her mother, saying **"It is an honour that I dream not of."** (We know this is a lie because that same night she tells Romeo that he needs to arrange their marriage. She has clearly looked at the Nurse and her mother, who were both married at the age of twelve, and has spent at least two years psychologically preparing for the same fate).

3. "Well, think of marriage now: younger than you,
Here in Verona, ladies of esteem,
Are made already mothers. By my count
I was your mother much upon these years
That you are now a maid. Thus, then, in brief;
The valiant Paris seeks you for his love."

Because Lady Capulet values status so highly, she uses status as her main argument to persuade Juliet. She tells her that daughters "younger than you" are already "ladies of esteem". Contrasting their age to "ladies" also suggests that this is the only way Juliet can gain status as an adult. She has also included an element of competition, pointing out that there are young rivals who are getting ahead of her socially.

Next, she points out that these younger "ladies of esteem" are "already mothers". She suggests that Juliet's age is old for a mother, and proves it by reminding her that she had Juliet herself when she was Juliet's age. The contrast with Capulet is stark. He has probably realised that this was a mistake in his own marriage and asks Capulet to wait "two more summers" till Juliet is sixteen.

Finally, she is abrupt and business like. When she tells Juliet about Paris, she doesn't bother to find attractive reasons to recommend him and marriage in general. Instead she coldly announces, "Thus, then, in brief". This tone implies that it is Juliet's duty to marry young, to immediately get pregnant and marry their choice of husband, Paris.

4. "This precious book of love, this unbound lover,
To beautify him, only lacks a cover: …
That book in many's eyes doth share the glory,
That in gold clasps locks in the golden story;"

When she does try to persuade Juliet to marry Paris she uses a fascinating metaphor of Paris as a "book". She invites Juliet to see herself as part of Paris's "golden story", but she is just the "cover". The repetition of "gold" emphasises the wealth and status he will provide for her. But the patriarchal point of the metaphor is that she is telling Juliet that women simply can't write their own story, they have no independence from the man they marry. She implies that a woman has no influence on how that story – the narrative of her life – will unfold. Therefore, the only sensible option is to choose a husband whose story will be most "golden". Her role is only "To beautify him", which is her route to status and wealth: she will then be able to "share the glory" with her husband.

Shakespeare wants us to understand that Lady Capulet represents all women who have been "sold" and abused in this way. They have to make the best of a terrible situation and turn it to their advantage.

5. "Therefore have done: some grief shows much of love,
But much of grief shows still some want of wit."

Her mother points out her "want of wit". It seems extraordinary that she suggests Juliet needs to ignore her emotions after the death of Tybalt just the previous day.

But Shakespeare also wants us to understand the consequence of the patriarchal control of women. He suggests that being married, and then becoming a mother so young, next watching so many of your children die, means that women become emotionally numb. Instead, they weigh emotions for their advantage – just this much "shows much of love" but too much shows "want of wit".

What makes this doubly cruel is that it is also probably a lie so soon after Tybalt's death. It is simply convenient to suppress this grief so that a new marriage to Paris can be carried out with the appropriate level of celebration. She can't afford for Juliet to ruin it with tears.

6. "We will have vengeance for it, fear thou not.
Then weep no more. I'll send to one in Mantua,
Where that same banish'd runagate doth live,
Shall give him such an unaccustom'd dram

That he shall soon keep Tybalt company:"

It's worth remembering that Shakespeare doesn't just want to criticise the patriarchal society in England, he wants to point out that in Catholic Mediterranean countries things are much worse. Here he develops the idea of the blood feud, where families don't just have occasional clashes, but organise assassinations across the generations.

He also chooses poison as a preferred means because the Italians, through the Borgia and Medici families were famous for it. This is also a way to discredit Catholicism. A Borgia had been Pope a hundred years before the play, and was soon succeeded by a Medici Pope, so the reference to poison points to the corruption of the Catholic church.

It also works thematically. Just as Mercutio's "plague on both your houses" becomes real with the plague which prevents Romeo learning that Juliet is not dead, so "one in Mantua" does provide "an unaccustom'd dram" that kills Romeo. But this of course also leads directly to Juliet's death, and so Shakespeare uses this to point out how much Lady Capulet is to blame for her daughter's death.

7. "Well, well, thou hast a careful father, child;
One who to put thee from thy heaviness,
Hath sorted out a sudden day of joy,"

As usual, Lady Capulet refuses to use Juliet's name as a way of emphasising her power over Juliet. She portrays the marriage falsely to Juliet. We know that Capulet has arranged the marriage at such speed to satisfy his "son" Paris, to whom he asks "like you this haste?" Lady Capulet tries to manipulate Juliet by suggesting her father's motive was to alleviate her "heaviness". The fiction also involves the patriarchal idea that she should be happy to have this marriage arranged for her.

When she describes the marriage, her sibilance therefore sounds sinister rather than soothing. Shakespeare uses it to emphasise that it is a "sudden day", so that we pick up it is much too "sudden". The ominous nature of this "haste" is also emphasised with the alliteration of "d", so we feel the full force of her lie, forcing her daughter into a marriage which would concern us even if she weren't married to Romeo.

8. "Ay, sir; but she will none, she gives you thanks.
I would the fool were married to her grave."

Shakespeare emphasises Lady Capulet's complete absence of compassion. He again uses irony, so that what she wishes for her daughter comes true – she is "married to her grave", dying next to her husband in her own tomb. This again emphasises how we are supposed to blame the parents for her death, more than the fact that she is a "fool" for committing suicide.

9. "Talk not to me, for I'll not speak a word. / Do as thou wilt, for I have done with thee."

Baz Luhrmann decided that this complete abandonment of Juliet was caused by her husband's violence. But there is no textual evidence of this. When characters are violent towards each other, Shakespeare makes them refer to this in their speech – if Shakespeare wanted Capulet to hit his wife, their dialogue would say so.

So, why is Lady Capulet so cold towards her only child? It could be that Shakespeare wants to use Juliet's complete abandonment by both parents, and then the Nurse's sudden advice to marry Paris, as a plausible explanation for Juliet's option of suicide. It could also be that Shakespeare points out that patriarchal marriage is dehumanising – a woman has to give up so much of her personality and identity to make it work, that their natural emotions are stunted. We are both horrified by Lady Capulet and pity her for the society which has damaged her.

10. "Ay, you have been a mouse-hunt in your time;
But I will watch you from such watching now."

It is no coincidence that these lines about Capulet's affairs happen as the parents are helping to prepare the feast for Juliet's wedding. Shakespeare is pointing out the one-sided nature of marriage, where the husband does not just get to possess the bride, her dowry, her virginity, her ability to breed heirs, but also feels perfectly entitle to carry on affairs on "a mouse-hunt". It is only now that her husband is nearly fifty, and she about twenty-six, that she will be able to prevent him having further affairs. She emphasises this with the word "now", perhaps meaning that without any children left at home she will at last be able to focus fully on her husband and finally achieve some status as an equal. He will no longer be able to get away with having affairs.

The phrase "mouse-hunt" also plays down the betrayal of these affairs. We see that Lady Capulet has had to shrug them off so that they don't cause her pain. But clearly they have, because she is now looking forward to them ending. It is possible that this is proof of love and jealousy, as Capulet imagines. But given everything we have seen so far, it is more likely that she sees it as proof of her increasing status. At twenty-six she is no longer just the "cover" to his "golden book", she is also the "gold clasps" that lock him into the marriage at last.

Top Ten Lord Montague and Lady Montague Quotes

1. "Thou villain Capulet! Hold me not, let me go."

Both Capulet and Montague protest but allow themselves to be held back by their wives. This partly suggests that their involvement in the feud is bravado, just like Sampson and Gregory.

2. "Thou shalt not stir one foot to seek a foe."

Lady Montague is given the last word here, which suggests she has some control over her husband. The fricative alliteration is also quite aggressive and forceful, which suggests she will be obeyed. Of course, if his threat to fight was simply bravado, then he intended to allow his wife to stop him fighting all along, and her power is an illusion!

3. "Who set this ancient quarrel new abroach?"

Montague doesn't really want to pursue the family feud, it is being done by the servants. Again, this suggests that servants aren't to be trusted even when they are really loyal. It adds to that air of looming threat that Shakespeare wants his audience to feel, and taps in to their real-world anxieties.

4. "Many a morning hath he there been seen,
With tears augmenting the fresh morning's dew,
Adding to clouds more clouds with his deep sighs;"

Shakespeare gives us Montague's sympathetic reaction to Romeo's tears because he knows that this will make a stark contrast to Capulet's treatment of Juliet's tears. Another implication is the role of the parent. Montague is allowing his son total freedom to stay out all night, and shut himself in his room in daylight. Does this make him a good parent, or one who lacks discipline and common sense?

5. "Could we but learn from whence his sorrows grow, / We would as willingly give cure as know."

Montague and his wife desperately want what is best for Romeo, but he is secretive and refuses to discuss his problems with them. Shakespeare will contrast how they are resolutely on Romeo's side. This differs from the Capulets, who have Juliet's long-term prosperity in mind, but care little about her feelings. Perhaps this is how society treats its boys better than girls.

6. "Not Romeo, Prince, he was Mercutio's friend;
His fault concludes but what the law should end,
The life of Tybalt."

Montague's appeal to the Prince possibly persuades him not to execute Romeo, but instead to banish him. We get some sense of him as a leader who is respected. Shakespeare builds on this when it is Montague's idea to build a golden statue, and Capulet then follows suit.

7. "Hold, take this letter; early in the morning / See thou deliver it to my lord and father."

Romeo feels tremendous loyalty to his father here. It is a mature act, to worry about how his parents will deal with his death. The injustice of the patriarchal society is revealed by the fact that the letter is addressed to his father, not both parents.

8. "Alas, my liege, my wife is dead tonight.
Grief of my son's exile hath stopp'd her breath.
What further woe conspires against mine age?"

Romeo's mother has died of grief. We can see this as a measure of how much she loved Romeo. A patriarchal reading would see this as the weakness of women – that effeminate instinct that Romeo criticised in himself. Perhaps patriarchal males would argue that Romeo's excessive love for Juliet is also effeminate, because it mirrors his mother's excessive love for him. Her death is also ironic – although she is the parent who loved him to excess, Romeo's suicide note is written to his father, not his mother.

9. "But I can give thee more, / For I will raise her statue in pure gold,"

Montague's final lines begin with six syllables which complete Capulet's preceding four syllable line. This shows them now in partnership and harmony. To emphasise this, the men both agree to build golden statues of the other's child.

10. "That whiles Verona by that name is known,
There shall no figure at such rate be set
As that of true and faithful Juliet."

Montague focuses on Juliet's faithfulness – what he is rewarding is her desire not to have sex with another man. In this case, she has killed herself rather than be with Paris or any other man. This of course is a very patriarchal view of her worth. The alternative would be to have an unfaithful Juliet still alive. Montague's gift implies that would be worse.

Top Ten Prince Quotes

**1. "If ever you disturb our streets again,
Your lives shall pay the forfeit of the peace."**

The Prince is not an effective ruler. Because order can only be restored at the end of a tragedy, Shakespeare needs him to be weak. So, the Prince points out that this is the third "brawl", and we know he therefore should have intervened much earlier, after the first. Then he threatens the next instigators with death, a complete over-reaction, given that in the three fights so far, no one has died.

2. "Immediately we do exile him hence."

The Prince's original threat was to execute both parties to the brawl, which is especially clear from the plural "your lives". But now that the streets have actually been disturbed by the two deaths of Mercutio and Tybalt, the Prince backtracks. This makes him appear both weak and favouring the Montagues.

**3. "But I'll amerce you with so strong a fine
That you shall all repent the loss of mine."**

He decides to fine both families, not because it is the right thing to do, but because he has suffered the loss of Mercutio, his relative. This implies his justice is not impartial or fair. We also wonder if the fine will fill the public purse and be used for Verona's citizens, or for himself. In any event, a civic fine would have been an excellent solution to the first brawl and might have proved to be the exact deterrent.

**4. "Come, Montague; for thou art early up
To see thy son and heir more early down."**

The wordplay of this contrast suggests the Prince is enjoying the moment when he tells Montague that his "son and heir" is dead. Montague has not just lost a son, but his only son, therefore his "heir". He is letting Montague know that he will have no son to whom to pass on his name, title and fortune.

5. "We still have known thee for a holy man."

Shakespeare plays with the idea of how much we should blame the Friar. We are convinced he is intelligent, but manipulative. We know that his plan is for the greater good of Verona, but that in the end he acts out of cowardice, leaving Juliet alone. We also know that neither lover would have died if he hadn't married them. The audience probably arrived at the play already believing him to be corrupt exactly as he is in the source poem. Shakespeare undermines this with the Friar's frequently wise advice.

But the Prince shares none of our doubts about the Friar, and can see only goodness in him. We might go so far as to see this as a dramatisation of how the Catholic church had too much influence over the country's rulers. We can certainly see this as proof of the Prince's ineffectiveness.

6. "See what a scourge is laid upon your hate, / That heaven finds means to kill your joys with love!"

The Prince clearly believes that Fate is being controlled by "heaven", by God. He grasps that the lovers' deaths have been part of God's plan as a punishment for the families' "hate". Again, he uses a contrast, pointing out the irony of God killing the children "with love" as a punishment for the parents' "hate". This crafting again suggests his relish at this punishment.

7. "And I, for winking at your discords, too/ Have lost a brace of kinsmen."

The Prince also believes that he is guilty of having been an ineffective ruler – "winking at discords" in the first and second brawls. Shakespeare uses the tragic deaths to restore order at all levels of society. This is a cathartic end to the intense emotions of the play, though the anxiety of Queen Elizabeth's lack of an heir is undiminished.

8. "All are punished."

Because a tragedy tries to alleviate feelings of despair at the end, through catharsis. Capulet and Montague agree to build a "golden statue" of each other's child as they put aside their "enmity". But we get a sense that for the Prince, this is beside the point. What really matters is that God has restored order by punishing everyone for their hubris, including himself. Through the Prince, Shakespeare suggests that his tragedy is not one where the hero battles with his fate. Instead, all the leading players in Verona's society have either died tragically or been the victim of their relative's tragic deaths. The tragedy and punishment are therefore directed at the ruling classes. Shakespeare uses this to hold a mirror up to his own society in England. Because he refuses to punish the Nurse and the Apothecary, unlike Brooke's source poem, we can also argue that just punishing the nobility is a deliberate choice.

9. "Go hence, to have more talk of these sad things".

The Prince voices Shakespeare's message here. Shakespeare wants the audience to look at the play as a mirror, and question their own society, especially its patriarchal structures, the roles of women and the idea of male honour.

**10. "For never was a story of more woe
   Than this of Juliet and her Romeo."**

Shakespeare also give the Prince the final words of the play. This helps to restore civic order to society within Verona, and emphasise the catharsis it provides. It also asks the audience to take the Prince's request "to have more talk" as not just a request of the character, but from Shakespeare himself.

Top Ten Minor Character Quotes

1. Paris: "Do not deny to him that you love me."

Shakespeare takes each character who will die and holds up their hubris to us, so that we can see their deaths as a tragic consequence of their arrogance. We frequently meet Paris in media res with Capulet. Capulet's conversation helps us infer that Paris is forthright and eager in marrying Juliet quickly. What tips this unseemly "haste" into arrogance is this line. When he tells her "Do not deny" we imagine he actually believes that she does love him. Because his society is so patriarchal, he would be an incredibly attractive match for any noble daughter. Because he is both handsome and young (where most wealthy husbands are older, as Capulet was), his experience must have been that other daughters have weighed him against the alternatives on offer, and been desperate to win his affection. He knows all this, but thinks this engenders real love. Shakespeare points out that this warped sense of self worth is inevitable in a society that values male status so highly, and female independence so slightly. This is why Fate kills him off.

2. "APOTHECARY: My poverty, but not my will, consents."

Unlike Brooke, Shakespeare doesn't kill the apothecary. He uses the servants to explore the whole of society and to ask for some level of social justice. The apothecary is a healer, and deserves to be able to make a living. However, he has to compete with the monasteries and friaries, with monks and friars who have no operating costs. This is why he is so poor. By drawing attention to this poverty, Shakespeare is tapping in to his audience's distrust of these Catholic institutions. Although only about 2% of the population were in religious service in the 1530s, these institutions owned 25% of all agricultural land, and a huge proportion of the country's wealth. Dissolution didn't give those lands to ordinary citizens, but it did open up many opportunities for individuals to start their own businesses without being undercut by the church. Romeo's appeal to social justice therefore celebrates Protestant England in contrast to Catholic Europe.

3. "Friar John: Where the infectious pestilence did reign / Sealed up the doors and would not let us forth."

As you know, Shakespeare himself may have secretly been Catholic. Here we find Friar John risking his life to help others in a household with suspected plague. Nobody else would go into such a house, and the occupants were forbidden to leave until they had contracted the disease and survived, or passed a quarantine period. Here were your chances of survival:

- **Bubonic plague** - 50% chance of death.

- **Pneumonic plague** – this infected the lungs. 90% chance of death

- **Septicaemic plague** - this infected the blood. 100% chance of death.

So, Friar John becomes a heroic figure, who also represents the good that many Friars did. He is a symbol of what the country lost with dissolution. He is also a clue that Friar Lawrence began with noble intentions, and was willing to risk personal criticism for marrying the lovers, before Romeo's hubris and killing of Tybalt made this impossible.

4. Paris: "Sweet flower, with flowers thy bridal bed I strew—".

It is tempting to see this moment as proof that Paris was genuinely in love with Juliet, just as Romeo was. This detail clutters the story of Romeo and Juliet's love, taking some of the focus away from their relationship. For this reason, many productions cut this scene.

But there is another way to look at this scene. It may be that Shakespeare has included it to show the patriarchal obsession with virginity, rather than the purity of love. When Paris strews "flowers" he is focused on her virginity, which he will never possess. We know that "flower" represents virginity, and Shakespeare gives this added weight through Paris's focus on the "bridal bed" where he would have taken that virginity. In this way, Shakespeare mocks this obsession with patriarchal control of virginity, and chooses this to be the moment when Paris will be killed.

5. "First Citizen: Down with the Capulets! Down with the Montagues!"

Its important to realise that the feud is disrupting the whole city. It is obviously well known, because the citizens know exactly which families are involved. That they are not taking sides, but opposed to both families, tells us something important about cities. In rural England, villages and farms are tied to the local land owner – usually a lord, and their family. In cities, citizens are able to live more freely, to choose their own fates. Cities don't just promise work, they offer independence and entrepreneurship. This is a departure from the Danvers Long feud which took place in small country towns, like Corsham in Wiltshire. By introducing the citizens' disapproval, Shakespeare is celebrating his London audience as citizens, proud of their independence in a world where their parents and grandparents possibly travelled less than ten miles from their home village or town.

6. "SERVANT: Perhaps you have learned it without book. But I pray, can you read anything you see?"

Shakespeare chooses the catalyst for the tragedy to be a servant who can't read. The servant realises the inadequacy of having to learn "without book" and would love to be able to "read anything you see". "Anything" conveys his sense of wonder at the freedom this would provide. Shakespeare is making a social point here about the need for literacy. It is an implicit criticism of Capulet that he has not made sure his servants can read, especially the males. By making illiteracy the catalyst which sends Romeo to his fate, Shakespeare points out that that illiteracy is a tragedy, and perhaps invites the rich members of his audience to think about correcting this in their own households.

7. "Nurse: And thou must stand by too and suffer every knave to use me at his pleasure!
PETER: I saw no man use you at his pleasure; if I had, my weapon should quickly have been out."

The Nurse complains to Peter that he has stood by while Mercutio, Benvolio and even Romeo insulted her. But her phrase for this insult is "use me at his pleasure". For Peter, as for the audience, this has a double meaning as sexual "pleasure". The Nurse, as usual, is unaware of her own innuendo.

Peter's reply is also innuendo. To the Nurse it means that he would have drawn his "weapon" to defend her. To Romeo and the audience, his innuendo means that if he had seen men "use [the Nurse] at his pleasure" he would have joined in. Although this is humorous, it contains a dark overtone. It reminds us of the dark overtones of the play and again links the male sexual exploitation of women to violence. The audience's laughter also makes them complicit in this, and it helps remind us of Shakespeare's focus, attacking patriarchal male abuse of women.

8. "CAPULET: How long is't now since last yourself and I / Were in a mask?
CAPULET'S COUSIN. By'r Lady, thirty years."

This quotation is important because it shows the social significance of this "mask". Capulet is throwing it to show off his wealth and influence, and he indicates to Paris that he is welcome to come – we don't get the sense that it is thrown in his honour. It is likely, however, that it is intended partly to showcase the eligibility and beauty of his daughter Juliet. Capulet certainly invites Paris to see "fresh female buds" at the ball, an indication that part of its purpose is to showcase available girls.

The other reason it is important is that it places Capulet's age near 50. Shakespeare wants us to know the great age gap between him and his wife, so that we can understand what a raw deal the young bride usually gets in the wealthy alliance brokered by her father. This helps us understand both Capulet's amazement that Juliet is not delighted at his choice of the youthful Paris, and Juliet's horror of being forced to marry an older man (because even twenty-five will seem ancient to a thirteen-year-old).

9. "PETER: O, I cry you mercy, you are the singer. I will say for you. It is 'music with her silver sound' because musicians have no gold for sounding."

In another scene which is often cut, Peter has to persuade the musicians to sing a funeral song for Juliet. The reason they object is that they have been hired to sing and play in the marriage procession, by Paris. Peter knows each musician by name, but mocks them for being poor. He points out that they must sing the song "music with her silver sound" as that is the closest they are going to get to wealth, they will never earn enough to be paid in "gold".

This humour helps us understand the importance of status. Peter feels he can mock the musicians because, even though he is a servant, his trusted position in the household makes him socially superior to the musicians who have less secure work. It may be that Shakespeare is asking his audience to consider the artists who perform for them, to treat them better. Or it may be a joke he himself is playing on his own musicians hired to perform during the play.

The scene acts as a comic counterpoint to the tragedy of Juliet's apparent death. Shakespeare usually provides humour as a way to contrast with the tragedy. There is also the political point that the poor don't have the luxury of indulging in their feelings – they simply have to do what is necessary to earn subsistence wages.

10. "FRIAR LAWRENCE: Go with me to the vault.

BALTHASAR: I dare not, sir;
My master knows not but I am gone hence,
And fearfully did menace me with death
If I did stay to look on his intents."

Shakespeare really liked the name Balthasar, and used it for a minor character in four of his plays. Balthasar was one of the three wise men to follow the star to Bethlehem and celebrate Jesus's birth.

His name is therefore a symbol of goodness. How is that goodness repaid here? Romeo asks Balthasar to wait and threatens him with death if he comes into Juliet's tomb. Balthasar "dare not" go in with the Friar, believing that Romeo really would "menace me with death". This moment adds to the Friar's sense of dread, and keeps death at the forefront of everyone's mind. But it is also unnecessary to the plot – the Friar could simply have passed by without seeing Balthasar. The only reason to include this incident is to reveal the precarious role of a servant. It is a subtle attack on the noble families and their attitude to their staff.

"BALTHASAR: As I did sleep under this yew tree here,
I dreamt my master and another fought,
And that my master slew him."

The effect of a master's control is so complete, that Balthasar has repressed the experience of seeing Romeo kill Paris, and tells himself that this was a dream. He persuades himself that he "did sleep" rather than just hide, because that will avoid having to bear witness to what he has seen. The master/servant relationship distorts reality, and so Shakespeare criticises it.

R PJ
2021 - Death
2020 - close relationships
2019 - Fate
2018 - Power
2017 - Family Honour
2022 - Marriage

Printed in Great Britain
by Amazon